PUZZLED

Charleston, SC
www.PalmettoPublishing.com

Puzzled
Copyright © 2023 by Pauline Smith Jensen

All rights reserved

No portion of this book may be reproduced, stored in a retrieval system, or transmitted in any form by any means–electronic, mechanical, photocopy, recording, or other–except for brief quotations in printed reviews, without prior permission of the author.

Paperback ISBN: 979-8-8229-1809-2

PUZZLED

Life Lessons Learned from Doing Puzzles

PAULINE SMITH JENSEN

AUTHOR'S NOTE

Throughout this book, I use the word **"PUZZLING"** as a verb to describe the process of assembling a puzzle.

I'd also like to comment briefly on the image I chose for this book's cover. During my family's second stay on New York's Long Island back in 1962-63, my father—a professor of speech and drama—was preparing a textbook entitled: *Skill in Reading Aloud.* In preparation for its publication, his publisher sent him to Greenwich Village on Manhattan Island to be photographed at an outlet called *Von Behr's Photography.* Daddy took me with him that day and the photographer insisted on taking my photograph, which Daddy allowed. I was only 16 years old at the time. In those days, photographers were only able to create black and white pictures. *Von Behr* took several photos of me, some with white backgrounds and some with black backgrounds—for contrasting effects.

As I contemplated different possibilities for the cover of this book, I chose the one with the black background for two reasons. First, it possessed a quality of mystery, intrigue, and is suggestive of pondering or reflection—something I hope this book will influence in readers. Second, the photograph was taken by the same man who took Daddy's picture for his book decades ago, so it seemed appropriate, special, and even perfect to use this particular photo and idea for *my* new book.

Daddy died in 1964, just two months after I graduated from University High School in Honolulu. My father was very good and kind to me and he and I were close. I was the youngest of his seven children. The year before he died—my senior year in high school—I was the only child still at home and the two of us would go to the beach three times each week. I cherish these and other memories I have with my father—and particularly during that last year before his passing, when my mother and I had him all to ourselves. Losing Daddy at such a young age has been an ongoing challenge throughout my life.

I'm confident my father would be pleased with my choice of photo for the cover of this book. I can hear him now saying my selection is *"Just the Ticket,"* a phrase I heard him use many times growing up. Who would have ever guessed I would find this photo and place it on the cover of my own book so many years later? This is just one of many things that makes life interesting, adventurous, unpredictable, and so worth living!

Thank you for taking time out to read this book; I am honored you would do so! I hope your journey reading this book will make you feel more excitement, motivation, and zest along your own life's adventurous pathways.

– Pauline Smith Jensen
Cedar Hills, Utah, USA
September 7, 2023

To my seven (7) children and thirty-one (31) grandchildren.

And especially to my fifth son and sixth child—Jordan Rex Jensen—who has, in his 44 years, climbed more mountains than most, and not just survived, but thrived. He is a shining example to me of humility, love, patience and perseverance and I am so proud to call him my son. As a doctor of education, professional writer, published author, and my son, Jordan was uniquely qualified and ideally suited to serve as my editor, proofreader, publication liaison, confidant, and support throughout the process of putting pen to paper and otherwise creating this book. I express to him my sincere gratitude for his many contributions to this project.

Table of Contents

Chapter 1: Introduction — 1

Chapter 2: Where Life and Puzzles Differ — 10

Chapter 3: Getting Started — 19

Chapter 4: Trial & Error — 25

Chapter 5: It May Fit, but is it Right? — 32

Chapter 6: Commitment & Consistency — 42

Chapter 7: Take a Break — 64

Chapter 8: Be Informed — 68

Chapter 9: The Power of Positive Affirmations or Turn it Upside Down — 77

Chapter 10: Now What? — 87

Chapter 11: From Fear to Faith — 94

Chapter 12: Final Thoughts — 102

Chapter 13: Maxims to Live By — 110

Appendix: Puzzle Picture Gallery — 116

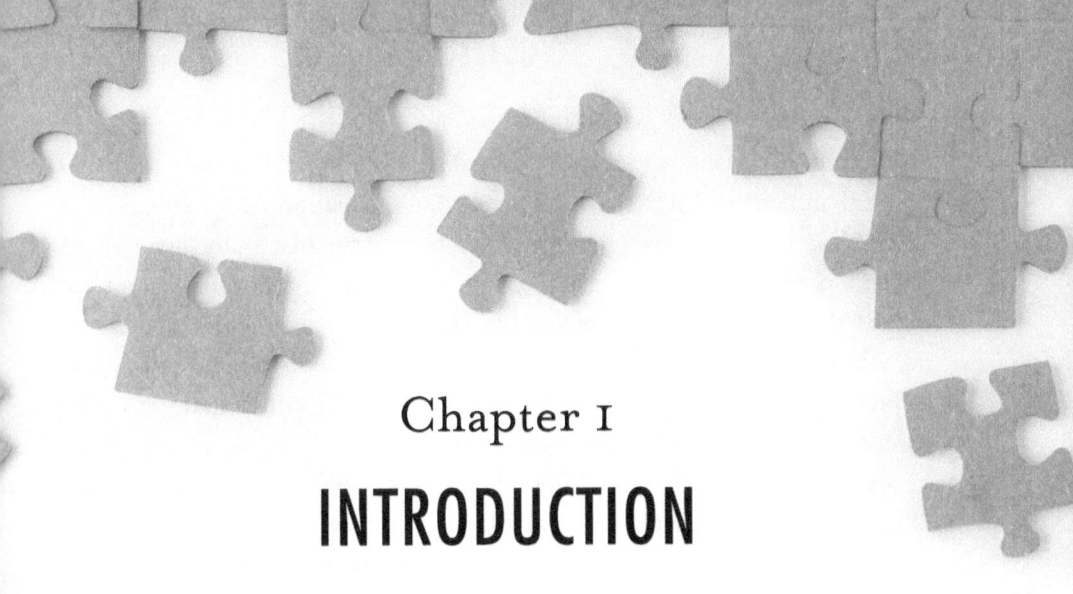

Chapter 1

INTRODUCTION

Why write another self-help book?

And why now?

Like most people, I've been through a lot in my life. Fortunately, some of our greatest lessons come from adversity. The best thing we can do for ourselves is to learn these hard lessons well enough that we gain the courage, insight, and determination to avoid repeating our failures. If we succeed in doing so, we become equipped with experience and wisdom that can, in-turn, be passed along to others who are coming up and trying to find their way in the world.

I began this project in 2020 as America—and the world-at-large—was passing through some very difficult times due to the COVID-19 pandemic. Stores and restaurants shut down, schools and churches closed, and millions of people were sick and dying all over the planet. Wearing masks was required and the population was encouraged to isolate and stay home. Folks over 70 were most vulnerable, so my children worried about me because I am a septuagenarian myself.

I've always been a social being who enjoys spending time with other people, so this "New Normal"—as the media was calling it—felt more like a "New *Ab*normal" to me. Add to this the looting, rioting, and other destruction occurring throughout major U.S. cities in conjunction with the political and cultural unrest which permeated our nation and it seemed like all hell had broken loose. I felt personally blessed because I am fortunate to live in a comfortable home in a very safe suburban neighborhood in a state (Utah) that was largely sheltered from the violence that poured out from my television screen. Nevertheless, the malaise was depressing to watch and seemed to add an air of generalized gloom to my life, which had grown increasingly isolated socially due to the lockdowns.

Amidst these challenges, I considered myself blessed that I knew how to crochet because it provided me with something productive to do while I watched television. A tradition of mine is to crochet an afgan for each of my grandchildren when they graduate from high school. I also enjoy crocheting little hats for newborn babies. Accomplishing this work made me feel better about all the time I spent watching the depressing news.

In addition to crocheting a lot during the lockdowns, I also read books, took walks, and made fudge and brownies to share with my friends and neighbors. These activities helped me maintain my sanity while serving others—something which has always brought me satisfaction and joy and helped me avoid becoming too self-absorbed. I've never been a great cook, but my children all survived and I do make a wicked batch of fudge! It makes me happy to be able to share this simple talent with others.

Meanwhile, a dear friend of 50-plus years sent me a puzzle, by Dowdle, called *North Shore*. You've probably heard of the "North Shore." It's located on the *windward* side of the Hawaiian island of Oahu, which has always held a special place in my heart because I grew up in Honolulu—on the *leeward* side of the island

The puzzle my friend sent me was an intricate and complicated design with 1000 pieces, which seemed like a tremendous challenge to me at the time. But knowing that my unique circumstances at *this* particular time in my life had gifted me with ample amounts of free time, I figured I had nothing to lose to give it a shot. It took me three-and-a-half weeks to complete and I confess I had a little help from my twin sons one Sunday afternoon.

North Shore nearing completion

PUZZLED

North Shore completed

As I reflected on the experience, I was surprised to discover how much I enjoyed working on *this* puzzle. It provided a lovely break and respite from my other activities and gave me something to work at and focus on during a time when I found myself troubled by how to productively utilize all my extra time at home. Because I enjoyed the work so much, I would find myself deeply absorbed in meaningful "FLOW"[1] states.

Once I was "in the [puzzle] zone," I would lose track of time, accomplish a great deal, and derive great satisfaction from my work. For instance, I recall one afternoon sitting down with the intention of spending 30 minutes working on a puzzle. I was shocked when I looked at the clock and realized I had been there for FIVE (5) straight hours! The satisfaction I experienced from finding and placing a puzzle piece was like "Pure Morphine" for me as my new hobby became positively addicting. Given this highly pleasurable experience with my *North Shore* puzzle, you won't be surprised to learn that I soon went out and purchased two more puzzles and quickly set to work assembling them.

As I worked on these additional puzzles, my mind became flooded with thoughts and ideas about all the metaphors that existed between assembling puzzles and living one's life. Indeed, I've never assembled a puzzle that hasn't taught and schooled me in a way that helps me to make sense out of my real-life experiences. These life lessons seemed sufficiently meaningful that my heart began to burst with desire to share what I was learning with others. At first, I experienced my share of "Writer's Block" and decided I would just keep doing more puzzles as I worked to further organize my thoughts and ideas for a book. But eventually I "Buckled Down" and set myself to the task of typing out a rough draft. Due to a variety of dips and delays in my life and schedule, it took me over a year to finish, but with focus and determination,

---

[1] FLOW is an academic term coined in the early 1970s by the psychologist Mihály Csíkszentmihályi to describe positive states of productive and pleasurable activity like those I experience "Puzzling." For more information, consult Csíkszentmihályi's work or buy Dr. Bruce H. Jackson's book: *Finding Your Flow: How to Identify Your Flow Assets and Liabilities—the Keys to Peak Performance Every Day.* Foreword by Stephen R. Covey.

I finally arrived at my goal. My youngest son, Jordan—a gifted writer and published author—then helped me make it across the finish line by serving as my editor, proofreader, and publication liaison.

I have always loved music and appreciated the power it has to positively influence my emotions. Every morning as I prepare for the day, I listen to music from CD's I've collected over the years. One day, before going to bed, I put a different CD in my machine, ready to listen to on the morrow. The CD was called *Front Row Center*—a collection of famous showtunes from Broadway hits sung by an actor and singer named Steve Amerson.

I'm a big fan of the *Old Musicals* and was deeply touched by the passion and pathos Amerson infused into his stirring album—so much so, in fact, that I shed tears listening to every song on his CD! From West Side Story's *Tonight*, *Something's Coming*, and *Somewhere*, to Disney's *Go the Distance* (from Hercules), the music and words deeply touched my heart and soul. As I listened to the song *Out There*, from Disney's *The Hunchback of Notre Dame*, I thought about a scripture from the New Testament:

> "For God hath not given us the spirit of *fear*; but of POWER, and of LOVE, and of a SOUND MIND."
>
> 2 Timothy 1:7

My sister Lynne, who died in 2003, sent me a card with this scripture when I returned to Brigham Young University to complete my formal college education in the late 1980s. I had begun my degree after graduating from high school in 1964, but after getting married in 1966, I took a 22-year hiatus to bear and raise my seven children. In 1988, when my youngest child was seven years old, I set a goal to graduate from college with my bachelor's degree before my first child beat me to it! As a right-brained creative thinker who is also somewhat dyslexic, I struggled in a very left-brain and analytical university environment. However, I've lived long enough to know that if I want authentic growth and real accomplishments, I have to be willing to tackle difficult tasks and endure patiently and persistently through any challenges that arise along the way. It took me five summers, but I eventually reached my goal and graduated with my bachelor's degree in elementary education in 1992—three years before any my kids received their degrees. It was a huge achievement for me! And it was enormously satisfying and fulfilling to see a significant goal through to completion despite facing huge obstacles along the way.

The concluding song on my CD was, *You'll Never Walk Alone*, from The Sound of Music wherein are sung those immortal words: "Climb every mountain, ford every stream, follow every rainbow, till you FIND *your* DREAM." My dream is to share with others my personal discoveries about life after living for over three quarters of a century in this world. In so doing, I hope to lift and inspire others to reach for and realize their own dreams.

I have discovered throughout this process that writing a book is not easy! Initially, I was holding back. But why? The obvious answer was procrastination; but that wasn't it. It was FEAR! Fear of failing. You see, my brother, Hyrum W. Smith, has written several self-help books that were very successful and it is intimidating working in the shadows of such success in my own family. Nevertheless, I know that if Hyrum were here (he passed away of cancer in 2019) he would tell me to stop comparing myself to him and passionately pursue my own dream with the recognition that my stories could prove just as valuable to others as his had been. I can almost hear him say to me with that big grin of his: "Pauline, what do you have to lose?" He is right, and I am glad I overcame my fear and pressed on until I achieved my goal.

In the early 2000s, I opened a variety shop called *Polly's Parlor* on Main Street in Monticello, Utah, USA, a rural community where I lived at the time. It was a new and challenging experience that required a leap of faith on my part. In commemoration of the event, my older brother Denis and his wife sent me a plaque that read:

> "The Jump is so frightening, between where I am and where I want to be, because of all I may become, I will close my eyes and leap."
>
> Mary Anne Rachmacher

I was deeply inspired by *this* message *then*. I am equally inspired by it *now*.

It is with gratitude and humility that I share with you the life lessons I have gleaned from doing puzzles—and living 77 years of life. I hope and pray it will bless your life and perhaps guide and inspire you to move forward to make YOUR *own* dreams come true, regardless of the unique life limitations and challenges you face. At the very least, I hope you'll be inspired to go out and buy yourself a puzzle and bask in the joy of the "Puzzling" process and benefit from the lessons you will discover for yourself along the way.

My journey in producing this book has been fascinating and a real joy! Throughout each chapter, I share stories and experiences from my own life to elaborate, explain, illustrate, or point out a specific life lesson. These stories and examples are designed to get YOU to think about how they relate to *your own* life stories and experiences.

To facilitate this process, I invite you to record your thoughts, feelings, and ideas in your personal diary or journal along the way. Doing so will greatly enhance your learning and maximize the value of embarking on this journey together. Similarly, don't hesitate to underline, highlight, and/or jot down ideas in the margins or on blank spaces available throughout the book. This will help you to truly make the book your own. It will also increase the book's value by the factor of your own collection of personal notes.

Only YOU can *decide* to grow and improve *your* life. It is my desire that you will let this book guide you through your own trials and tribulations to a higher, nobler, and more positive and productive way of living that empowers you to become all you are capable of becoming.

I hope you will be pleased with the results at the end of your own journeys throughout life. More importantly, may you ENJOY *the* JOURNEY all along the way!

Chapter 2
WHERE LIFE AND PUZZLES DIFFER

Significant parallels exist between the art and science of successfully assembling a puzzle and the philosophy of building a great life. Throughout this book, I compare the "Puzzling" experience to the daily grind of life—including the highs (successes and victories) and lows (disappointments and failures) that accompany life. In the process, I will walk you through the necessary steps to forge ahead through your own puzzling life events in ways that are positive, realistic, logical, and enjoyable.

In any journey or adventure, it is usually helpful to have a map. Below is a 7-step roadmap for puzzle assembly *and* living a good life. Accompanying these seven steps are seven "WHAT" questions to ask yourself along the process of enacting each step.

Step 1. **Decide**..................What do you really want most?
Step 2. **Set Goals** ....What intermediate steps are required?
Step 3. **Make a Plan** ....What daily tasks will accomplish intermediate steps?
Step 4. **Get to Work** ....What are you waiting for?
Step 5. **Evaluate**....................What needs to be improved?

Step 6. **Remember**........................What have I learned in the past that can help me now?
Step 7. **Retool**............................What else needs doing to get what I want most?

As we journey through this book together, I encourage you to keep these seven, basic steps in mind. Each chapter that follows will implicitly "Fill-in-the-blanks" to expand further on how you can put these basic steps into action to bring you great joy and fulfilment.

My time is precious. I know that your time is equally as valuable. With this in mind, my goal is to provide you with information and clarifying stories that will lift and edify in the short time we have together. Before highlighting the similarities between assembling puzzles and living the good life, it's important to highlight *one* key difference between the two.

When you purchase a puzzle, you generally select it because you like the picture on the box. You probably also chose it because of the number of pieces. Common sense suggests you probably shouldn't choose a 1000-piece puzzle on your first attempt. In life, our first effort is definitely not walking. We first learn to open our eyes, then roll over, and one day make it to our knees. Only then can we learn to crawl, which typically precedes walking. Likewise, your first puzzle experience should be small, with minimal pieces and a simple picture to follow. If you question the validity of that last statement, remember this: *if something is too difficult, we become afraid and discouraged.*

> **If something is too difficult, we become afraid and discouraged.**

When we succeed at something, it lifts us up and moves us forward to higher possibilities. Success tends to invigorate our minds and boost our self-esteem. Failure, on the other hand, can lead to frustration and discouragement as it stifles our momentum and halts our progress. Failure is not, of course, always bad because adversity can be a great teacher, as you will see when you undertake your first puzzle. But if you try and attempt something too difficult in the beginning, you unwittingly set yourself up for frustration, discouragement, and perhaps even failure.

When you set out to assemble a puzzle, you know exactly how it should look when it is finished. No matter how immense the challenge, or how hard or long it might take to assemble it, you always know that *in the end*, it is supposed to look just like the picture on the box.

Ancient Egypt puzzle completed

Real Life is different.

Unlike a puzzle, it is impossible to clearly see the end results when you are just starting out. You are born, learn, and make choices, but no matter what your plans, aspirations, or dreams might be, *Life Happens*, and you are not always guaranteed the end results you may have initially been aiming for.

We can have a genuine, wonderful vision and plan of what we want our lives to be, and then life brings unexpected challenges and problems that can seriously alter our view of how things should or *ought* to be. The important thing is to realize that a different path than we originally envisioned can be ok. The key is to maintain a positive attitude and never give up trying to make the best of things. As the old saying goes: "When Life gives you Lemons, make Lemonade!"

After all… lemonade is *delicious*!

Having a clear understanding of what life is all about makes it easier to traverse all the tributaries we inevitably take as we sail down the River of Life. Here are just a few variables that affect our lives, some of which we may have little or no control over.

- **Physical make-up**
- **People that come into our lives**
- **Circumstances of where we live**
- **Health**
- **Opportunities for education, or lack thereof**

When I was eleven years old, my mother enrolled me in a modern dance class. Growing up in Honolulu, Hawaii, the majority of my friends and classmates were Asian. My legs were very long and I was embarrassed that I was the only one in the entire class who could not touch the floor without bending my knees. Gratefully, rather than seeing this as a terrible, horrible thing, I recognized that most of my classmates had longer torsos and shorter legs. Of course it was easier for them to touch their toes without bending their knees!

Similarly, my height gave me an advantage in activities or games where being tall was an asset.

> **A big part of life involves discovery and then making choices based on our discoveries.**

For my 5th and 6th grade years, I attended a school called *Hanahauoli*, which in Hawaiian means "Happy Work." Every year the school organized and presented an Olympics. We were allowed to choose the sport we wanted to participate in and spent weeks preparing to do our best. Guess what I excelled in? Drum roll..........the *High Jump*! My Asian friends couldn't come close to the heights I achieved. A great *Discovery* was made: *Different does not mean defective.*

> **Different does not mean defective.**

I learned that we all have gifts unique to our physical and genetic make-up. Lamenting what I *couldn't* do was counterproductive. I could find more success by focusing on what I *could do*. Common sense will tell you that if you have a football player's build, perhaps dreaming of being the fastest runner in the world might not be the best idea. Conversely, if you are born with a slight frame and small bones, fantasizing about being a professional football player might not be wise either.

My point is that my original desire to one day be an amazing dancer was incongruent with what my body was designed for and capable of attaining. There is a saying that says, "*Don't Kick Against the Pricks.*" Instead, learn what your gifts and talents are, build on them, and discover the joy of blessing others' lives with what you have to give. And just for the record, wherever you may not excel, someone else does, and they can bless your life with *their* talents, just as you can bless their lives with *your* gifts.

Another life variable involves the circumstances where you live. As I mentioned earlier, I grew up in Honolulu, Hawaii. When I was going into 8th grade, my Father, who was head of the Speech Department at the University of Hawaii, embarked on a Professor Exchange with a Mr. Scanlon from New York. This meant that Daddy and Professor Scanlan exchanged jobs and homes for a year; and their families went with them. Wow! What an education and eye-opening experience that was! Talk about a lot of "firsts" in my life. It was the first time I had ever:

- **Ridden a bus to school.**
- **Endured really COLD weather.**
- **Seen and experienced SNOW.**
- **Experienced a non-Asian majority in the community**

As a little girl growing up in Hawaii, Mother used to defrost our freezer with an ice pick. She would put the shavings in a bowl and tell me: "This is what snow looks like." I couldn't imagine such stuff all over the ground! Well, I got to see plenty of snow on Long Island. I quite liked making snow balls and shoveling sidewalks, but enduring the cold temperatures was another matter. As my father observed how I detested and suffered in the cold weather, he started calling me his little *Hot House Plant*—because my thermostat was set at tropical. I didn't learn until years later that the key to beating the cold was layering your clothes. To this day, I still don't like the cold!

Aside from the extreme weather change, the second most interesting challenge and adjustment involved culture shock. In Hawaii, all my friends and teachers had been, kind, non-aggressive, soft spoken, and gentle Asians. The community and culture on Long Island was a different story! It's not that they were bad people; it's just that their temperament and dispositions were a lot different than the Asians I grew up with in Honolulu.

During our time on Long Island, I met a wonderful friend on the bus on the first day of school who observed that I rolled down my white bobby socks. She told me that in New York they don't roll socks down and I would be ridiculed if I didn't make the switch. She saved my life! We are still good friends to this day. Thanks to cell phones, we keep in touch regularly.

I learned a great deal during my time on Long Island. One of the most important lessons I learned was the importance of hands-on experience when it comes to understanding different cultures. Reading about other cultures is not enough!

So, what are the main ingredients in living a happy, successful, and meaningful life? I believe they are FAITH and HOPE. Without hope for a better, brighter, and more rewarding *tomorrow*, it is hard to feel motivated today. Having hope that our lives can and should be happy, successful, and meaningful help us to develop faith, which in turn empowers us to take actions that will lead us to realize our hopes. I define Faith as: *Action based on True Principles*.

Faith is Action based on True Principles

To illustrate this definition, consider the following example: I'm reading a book in the living room and the sun is setting, making it more and more difficult to read the words. The light switch to illuminate the room is about 12 feet away. I realize that I need to turn a light on. I know without question that if the switch was turned to ON, I would have light. However, no matter how much I need or want there to be light, it's not going to happen unless I physically get out of my chair, walk over to the switch, and make it happen (Action based on True Principles).

Whether we admit it or not, we all live by faith to one degree or another every day. We get in our car each morning in faith that we will get to a certain destination at a given time without mishap or accident. The key point, of course, is that we don't get there *until* we take action. Merely believing the car will get me there won't make it happen. I have to DO something to make it a reality. Thus, if we want to get somewhere, we approach the freeway with faith, not fear. Fear stops our ability to move forward. Faith ensures progress.

Another variable that is sometimes beyond our control is our physical health and well-being. For example, when I was 15 years old, I woke up one Sunday morning with a terrible pain in my stomach. At Church the pain became even worse. I couldn't endure it any longer and went to the ladies' room where there was a bench I could lie down on. Evidently, I was white as a sheet because a woman came into the restroom, saw me lying on the bench, and immediately scurried off to the chapel to summon my Mother. Mother took one look at me and was deeply concerned. Fortunately, our family doctor was in the chapel and Mother immediately brought him to examine me. Two hours later I was on the operating table having my appendix removed. It is my understanding that complete removal is the only cure for appendicitis.

WOW! Did I ask for this malady to spring up so quickly and unexpectedly? Was it part of *my* life's plan? Of course not! But that's okay because remember... *Life Happens*! But with these unplanned and unexpected turns, many lessons are learned which add positively to our education and perspective. Such times often teach us empathy, patience, understanding of others, and a perspective that can only be gained through enduring hard things.

When I got married in 1966, I had two years of college under my belt. During my third year I became pregnant. From about age 13, my greatest desire was to be a wife and mother. For me, motherhood was a higher priority than finishing college. In my view, raising my children was the most important assignment I would ever undertake in this world, so I dropped out of school.

Twenty-one (21) years and seven children (including a set of twins) later, I decided I wanted to finish my bachelor's degree. As a young child answering questions on demographic surveys, it had always meant a great deal to me to declare that both my parents were college graduates. I wanted my children to be able to say the same about me. There is a time and season for everything. I made the right decision to leave school when I did; and I also made the right decision to *return* to school when I did.

Assembling a puzzle, in my opinion, is one of the purest experiences you can have that parallels those steps and actions that can also help you to create your best life possible. I invite you to learn the steps to follow and then incorporate FAITH in your choices.

The remainder of this book addresses where puzzles and life lessons collide.

Chapter 3
GETTING STARTED

As you probably already know, different sides of our brains work in different ways. The left side of the brain controls the analytical processing of information. It is where we compute math, construct language, and figure out how to assemble or operate something—like learning how to drive a car or building something out of LEGOs. The right side of our brains is where our creative juices flow. It is responsible for art, music, and the generation of innovative ideas.

Most people tend to gravitate more strongly to one side over the other. For example, I am predominately *right-brained*, meaning I am naturally *more* creative and *less* analytical. However, we all use both sides of our brain, and the best results usually come from a balanced use thereof.

An example of this is beautifully illustrated when we sing a song. Have you ever stopped to analyze how and why you are able to remember the words to a song you learned as a child? It is because a song requires the concurrent use of both sides of our brain. The words involve our left brain, while the music is processed in our right brain. Without words, a song is just music. Without music, a song is just a poem. While instrumental music and poetry are wonderful in their own right, there is something extra special when you bring them together to form a lyrical song. When both sides of our brain work together in a concerted manner, greater outcomes are produced.

When I was in 7th grade, I had no knowledge of left versus right brain. All I knew was that memorizing information to be regurgitated on a test was difficult for me. However, I discovered if I created a melody to go with the words, I retained the information much more successfully! The tunes I concocted with my right brain were usually little more than a "beat or chant," but it made the words stick.

While studying the northwestern United States, my teacher required that we memorize the names of four different dams. In the eternal scheme of things, I didn't see any value in memorizing this information, but since it was bound to appear on a test, I knew I better be prepared. So, I put the four dams into a little chant with a beat (today you might refer to it as a rap). And do you know that after more than 60 years, I still remember the names of those four dams (Mica, Arrow,[2] Duncan, and Libby)! They are indelibly imprinted on my mind. It is certainly not information crucial to my ability to survive or function in real life (I don't even remember in which states they are located). The point is: I own this information because I used both sides of my brain in the memorization process.

Selecting a Puzzle

When selecting a puzzle, I encourage you to engage both sides of your brain. As your left brain analyzes the size, number of pieces, and assembling location, the right brain can consider the colors, subject matter, and related emotions. As both sides of your brain work together, you can pick the ideal puzzle to assemble at this point in your life. The selection process involves the following:

---

[2] The name of the High "Arrow" Dam has been changed and is now known as the "Keenleyside" Dam.

- Subject matter
- Puzzle dimensions (size and number of pieces)
- Puzzle shape
- Visual picture as shown on the box
- Colors involved
- Emotional connection (or lack thereof) that you *feel* about the puzzle
- Other reasons behind your choice (nostalgia, memories, subject matter, colors, etc.)

A puzzle of the U.S. Capitol I completed. I chose to assemble this puzzle because I love my country and was drawn to the beautiful colors, hues, and reflections in this particular piece.

Getting Started

You just walked into your home with your selection. Now you must decide exactly where you want to assemble it. Why is this important? Because it needs to be placed where it can remain without interrupting family functions while providing you with ample time to complete the puzzle and enjoy the process at your own pace.

As a mother with seven children at home, I was feeding nine people three times a day, so the dining room table would not have been a viable option at that point in my life. However, we had a beautiful hexagon-shaped table in our family room which proved to be "just the ticket" (as my father would say). This option allowed the entire family to see it, participate in its assembly, and watch it progress to completion. It was in a safe place and if it took several weeks to complete that was ok; our goal was to enjoy the puzzle, not to see how fast we could assemble it. Sometimes cousins or friends stopped by and would enjoy sitting with my children to work on the puzzle for a while. It proved to be a great activity for conversation and bonding.

At Christmas time I would alert Santa as to what kind of puzzle to put under the tree. It grew into a wonderful tradition such that Christmas was not complete without our family receiving a new puzzle on December 25th. For the rest of the holidays—and sometimes beyond—anyone could sit down any time they wished, for as short or long a period as they liked, and simply enjoy making a contribution to the family puzzle. We all experienced satisfaction when the puzzle began to gradually come together. It's a special sense of fulfillment that leaves you feeling delighted and content. You've probably heard the phrase "Try it; You'll like it!" I've found this saying to be especially true when it comes to puzzles!

Steps to Assembling a Puzzle

Now that you've selected the puzzle you want to do and decided *where* you are going to assemble it, it's time to begin the puzzle itself. The next few steps may seem unnecessary to mention because they are basically common sense, but you'd be amazed at how many folks who are new to puzzling fail to follow these basic steps and end up feeling frustrated, overwhelmed, and unhappy in their puzzling experience as a result. This may lead them to not complete their puzzle and stop trying new puzzles in the future, which in my opinion would be a tragedy because they would be missing out on so much fun, enjoyment, satisfaction, and joy!

STEP 1: **Open up the box and dump out the pieces.**

STEP 2: **Turn all the pieces right side up.**

STEP 3: **Separate out all the edge pieces.**

The edge pieces are the easiest to find because no matter what the shape of the piece, one side is always straight (unless the puzzle itself is round or oval shaped, in which case they will be curved). My Mother taught me to make my brain save my legs. With this philosophy in mind, I would put together all the edge pieces first, according as colors dictate, while regularly looking at the picture on the box for guidance and verification. Putting together the edges first is like laying the foundation of a house. It provides a framework that provides perspective on the overall size and scope of the puzzle. It also offers a sense of direction and order.

STEP 4: **Put all similar colors into like groups (e.g. sky, forest, water, grass, house, etc.).**

Experience has taught me that once the edges are all assembled, it may be tempting to work inward from there, and if that is your preference then go for it! However, you may find it easier and more satisfying if you focus instead on assembling groups of the same basic color (e.g. sky, forest, water, grass, house, etc.). This method creates clusters of the puzzle you can fit inside the edges as the assembly evolves.

All along the way, don't be shy about looking at the picture on the puzzle box; that's what it's there for! Advanced puzzlers may want to try their luck assembling a puzzle without looking at the box, and that is fine if your focus is to undertake an extra challenge. Just remember that doing it that way will indeed be more difficult!

STEP 5:   Fill in the blanks until the puzzle is complete.

This is the hardest part because there will be many instances where you will face challenges, difficulties, roadblocks, frustration, and perhaps even discouragement along the way, especially if your puzzle has a thousand pieces or more. This final step is simply stated (or written) but not always easily accomplished. As such, the rest of this book will focus on how to overcome any and all obstacles that may arise along your journey towards completing a puzzle and/or successfully confronting adversity in your life.

U.S. Capitol puzzle in process

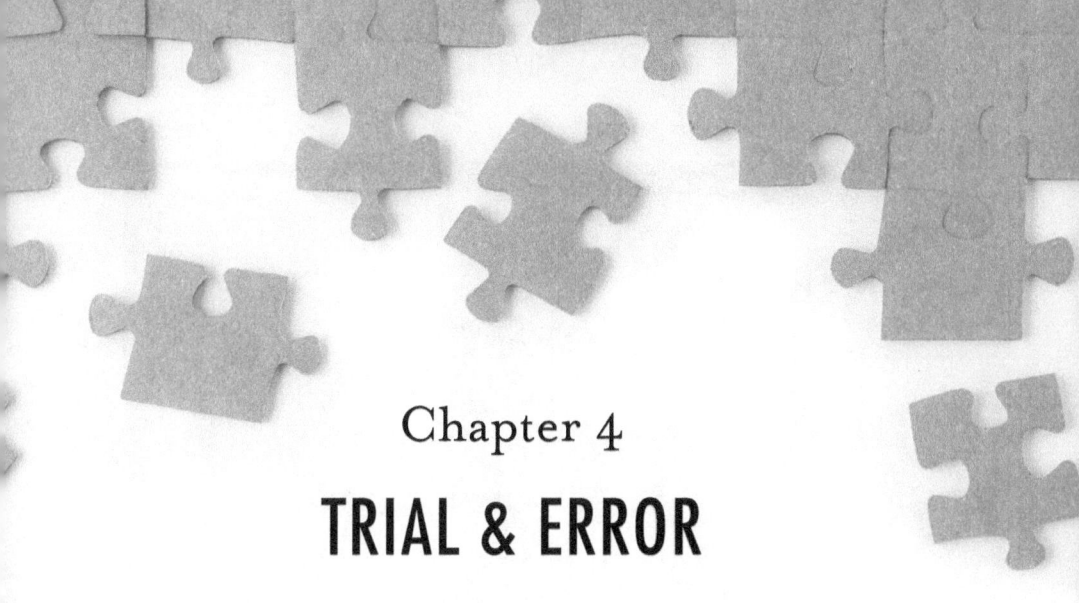

Chapter 4
TRIAL & ERROR

We have a tendency to believe what we see in print, be it a road sign or newspaper. The notion goes that if it's in print, it must be true! Once, I purchased a Puzzle entitled: "Grand Canyon." I knew the minute I looked at the picture that it was *not* the Grand Canyon in Arizona, but rather a photograph of *Monument Valley* in UTAH. I used to live a couple hours drive to the north of Monument Valley, in Utah, and have been there many times; so I know what it looks like!

It was a bit discombobulating to have the words tell me one thing and my eyes tell me something else—a clear case of "misinformation" to be sure. Frustration and mixed emotions ensued from this confusion between what my eyes knew to be true and what the words on the box were clearly communicating. The visual contradiction confused me enough that I felt like I needed to get a second opinion to validate what I assumed was true.

Grand Canyon (*Monument Valley*) puzzle poster

To obtain this validation, I texted a photo of the puzzle poster to a couple of my sons, David and Joseph, to get their opinion. They both verified that I was correct in my assessment. Why did this matter to me? Well, I actually lived in New York my eighth and eleventh grade years, where the landscape is drastically different from Utah, although New York City does have its own version of canyons made out of towering skyscrapers!

If one of my classmates from New York—who had never been to Monument Valley—were to purchase this puzzle, they would likely believe that the puzzle actually was a picture of the Grand Canyon. They might be convinced for years, or perhaps even the rest of their lives that Monument Valley is the Grand Canyon, even though it is not true. How often do we get hooked into believing what we read in print or see on television or the Internet?

Grand Canyon
(*Monument Valley*) in process

Grand Canyon
(*Monument Valley*) completed

The world in 2023 is full of chaos. From earthquakes, floods, fires, tornadoes, and hurricanes to misinformation, outright deception, and political and cultural unrest. Knowing my puzzle was blatantly mis-labeled and mis-represented is not going to drastically threaten me or change my individual world or how I live each day, but it was a reminder of how dangerous published falsehoods can be, especially when they come from institutions to which we look for guidance, leadership, and protection. History is full of entire populaces who have been bamboozled by institutional propaganda, and the results have often been dangerous, if not deadly or genocidal.

This "Puzzle Propaganda" was a good reminder that I should not believe everything I read in newsprint or watch on televised news programs. It reminds me of a story my parents told me when I was a youth. It's called "The Boy Who Cried Wolf" and was originally made famous by the great Greek storyteller Aesop. You are likely already familiar with the story: a shepherd boy is tired and bored, so he decides to put out a signal to the townspeople that a wolf is threatening the sheep. The good folks of the town come rushing to his aid only to discover that the boy was just teasing. The boy laughed and laughed as he watched the townsfolk fall for his trick. They, however, were not amused.

Sadly, as we sometimes foolishly do in our own lives, the boy decided to do the same dumb thing a *second* time—and again the townspeople unnecessarily rushed to his aid. At this point, the good folks of the town were pretty irritated to have been summoned *twice* only to be tricked by the foolish youth. As fate would have it, one evening, a wolf really did appear to threaten the sheep, but when he sounded the alarm, no one came. Why? Because the townspeople were convinced it was just another false alarm. The boy had lost their trust, and the sheep were unnecessarily devoured as a result.

Trust is one of the greatest qualities any of us can ever earn from another person or group of people. Your word is your bond; it is the highest form of integrity. Honesty is an important quality and character trait and the only true elixir for deception and misinformation.

Another lesson I have learned along these lines is that the only source of Truth I can know and absolutely trust comes not from human beings but from God. I was blessed to be raised in a home where my parents taught me to pray. Through my own experiences, I discovered that God does answer prayers. Thus, when I ask God if something is true, He can guide and direct me with His Holy Spirit through personal revelation that can guide me, protect me, and help me find inner peace. I don't see angels or hear voices, but when I ask sincerely and in faith, I do receive peace in my heart if something is true, and conflicted feelings if it is false.

Like everyone, I have made some choices in my life that have resulted in pain and sorrow, but because of my Faith in God I have only been wounded—not destroyed. Adversity does indeed teach magnificent lessons. I have a plaque hanging in my kitchen which reads: *You can Do the Impossible, because you have been through the Unimaginable.*

> "You can do the Impossible because you have been through the Unimaginable."
>
> Christina Rasmussen

Right above this thought is another message which states: *Let your Faith be Bigger than your Fears.* I read these gems several times a day and they remind me I can conquer whatever may come my way in an attempt to deceive me or hinder my progress.

> **Let Your FAITH be Bigger than Your *fears*.**

Now, back to other things the "Grand Canyon" (*Monument Valley*) puzzle taught me. Aside from lessons learned before I even attempted to put the puzzle together, I quickly discovered this to be an unusually difficult puzzle to conquer. In evaluating what made it harder than other puzzles, I realized two things. First, many pieces were the same color and otherwise had a similar appearance. Second, every interior (non-edge) piece had the same basic shape. They were not identical, just very similar. That is why I call this Chapter "*Trial and Error*," because in most cases finding a perfect fit was a hit-and-miss experience involving a lot of guessing.

Often a puzzle piece *seemingly* fits nicely, but is actually in the wrong place. It often took many attempts (and failures) before I found the precise fit. Along the way, I would often pick up a piece feeling confident it would fit, only to discover it did not. This kind of experience causes you to second guess your own perception, and past experience and expertise doesn't seem to help much.

Life can be a lot like my experiences with this puzzle. As we journey through life, it is not uncommon to feel angry, frustrated, discouraged, or even feel like giving up. Have you ever felt like your life is a continuous stream of trials and errors? No matter what your goal or target, you just can't seem to hit the sought-after bullseye? At such times we can benefit from having a positive attitude whereby by consciously *choose* to always see our glass as being half-full, rather than half-empty—regardless how difficult things become. This is, of course, much easier said than done. But in my experience, the principle proves perpetually productive.

I experience indescribable feelings of accomplishment and joy when I persevere to overcome difficult challenges. These positive feelings accompanied my completion of the very difficult Grand Canyon (*Monument Valley*) puzzle. For this reason, I encourage you to embrace your opportunities to do difficult things, whether it involves assembling a challenging puzzle, undertaking an ambitious and worthwhile project in your family, career, or personal life, or solving a difficult personal, professional, or relationship challenge. So go ahead; don't be afraid – DO THAT REALLY HARD PUZZLE – it will teach and prepare you for really hard things you will inevitably face in your life.

After completing the Grand Canyon (*Monument Valley*) Puzzle, I decided to frame it as a means of celebrating my accomplishment—and make no mistake: it was an accomplishment because is was so challenging; and overcoming difficulties is always satisfying, fulfilling, and worth celebrating!

Now that my puzzle is framed, I get to celebrate it again every time I walk past it in my home, although I confess I ended up giving it to one of my grandsons to spruce up his apartment décor at college; but for me, that was something to celebrate as well!

In conclusion, remember: *Don't always believe everything you see in print or on the news.* As President Ronald Reagan liked to say: *Trust; but verify.*[3]

---

[3] Reagan was introduced to the term by Suzanne Massie, an American scholar of Russian history.

> Don't always believe everything you see in print or on the news. "Trust, but verify!"

Truth is always best, even if it is bad news. When you take a cross country trip, it's comforting to have signs giving you directions and warning you of dangers ahead. Living in Utah, I have many experiences driving up steep, circuitous mountain roads that rise to elevations where snowfall is an ongoing threat throughout the winter. One road in particular, which I have driven on hundreds of times throughout my life, is considered by road experts to be among the most dangerous roads in the United States as judged by the number of auto accidents and deaths that occur on its precarious stretches. One day, as I set off to drive this particular stretch of road, I was grateful to see a warning sign that said: "*Dangerous winter roads ahead, proceed with caution.*" After receiving this warning, I made the decision to postpone my trip until the following day in the name of caution and safety. I'm glad I did because the next day I was able to travel more safely and arrive at my destination without mishap. Let's face it: *Life Happens and We Must Deal with it*. But it sure helps to have accurate information to guide us along the way!

> Life Happens and We Must Deal with It.
> *But it sure helps to have accurate information!*

Chapter 5
IT MAY FIT, BUT IS IT RIGHT?

Poster of Tuscan Courtyard puzzle

Aware of my love for puzzles, my daughter Jessie gave me this gem for Mother's Day. I've been to Italy twice and the scene brought back a multitude of special memories of my time there with my oldest sister, Ruth, who passed away in 2015. Remember, the first rule of selecting a puzzle is to choose one you really like, or are otherwise drawn to. The more enthusiastic you are about the puzzle you are assembling, the more you will enjoy the process. For me, this puzzle was worthy of being "Mod Podged" and framed rather than being disassembled and returned to the box after completion. For those who may be unfamiliar with the term, "Mod Podge" is a water-based sealer that is used to "glue" an assembled puzzle together. After being "Mod Podged," a puzzle serves as a picture or portrait and can be hung in one's home or on an office wall.

As I dumped the pieces onto my dining room table and began separating colors and searching for edge pieces, I wondered what lessons I might learn from assembling it. I had already gleaned a bushel of truths from previous puzzle encounters that helped me be successful, and I felt as though maybe I had learned all there was to learn from puzzling. But to my surprise and joy, I discovered there was still plenty left for me to learn as I continued working new puzzles, beginning with this one.

Some of the most important and valuable lessons you learn in your life come from mistakes you make along your way—assuming, of course, that you actually learn the lesson and avoid making similar mistakes in the future. Humble, self-aware puzzlers are transparent; when they make a mistake, they own up to it, make adjustments and changes where necessary, and proceed forward charting a wiser course moving forward. Prideful, non-aware puzzlers become truly *puzzled* along their journeys as they continually repeat the same mistakes, unnecessarily suffering unpleasant consequences over-and-over again.

The first step in CHANGE is recognizing (and admitting to yourself and, where necessary, to others) that you actually made a mistake. Then comes the penitence involved in fixing your mistakes. Step three is to take those necessary actions required to avoid repeating the mistake wherever possible. This may involve self-discipline, hard work, and where necessary, help from others.

You know you've made a mistake when the outcome is frustrating, dissatisfying, counterproductive, time wasting, painful, or leaves you feeling empty and unfulfilled. Such feelings are signals that you need to make necessary adjustments if you are going to get better, more desirable results in the future.

While assembling this puzzle, my first mistake became clear after putting together the pieces on the top left side where the cypress trees stood next to a building.

Tuscan Courtyard in process

Overall, I was pleased with my efforts up to this point. I had already learned from past encounters that when two pieces fit together effortlessly, I can rest assured I got it right. If it has to be forced, it's usually in the wrong place. I figuratively patted myself on the back and silently said in my mind, "Well Done." So far, every piece had slipped comfortably together. As I'm prone to do when working on a puzzle, I frequently look at the picture on the box to verify the accuracy of my efforts. However, after gazing back and forth multiple times from the picture on the box to the actual puzzle, I noted that something wasn't quite right. The trees in my puzzle were higher than was shown in the picture. It was a slight and subtle difference, not more than an inch, but the truth was that my assembly was wrong. How could this be? The pieces fit together nicely and easily and duplicated the trees exactly as portrayed on the box, so how could this have happened? Of course, when it's wrong in one place, havoc ensues in other parts of the puzzle as well. This, in-turn, leads to mismatches throughout the entire landscape. When that happens, there is only one satisfactory course of action if you want the puzzle to be assembled correctly: you must *undo* your mistake and then *redo* the pieces correctly.

There is no other way!

Often in life we make mistakes which must be corrected in order to achieve the outcomes we seek. The famous Christian apologist and juvenile fiction author, C.S. Lewis, once explained it this way:

> "We all want progress. But progress means getting nearer to the place where you want to be. And if you have taken a wrong turning, then to go forward does not get you any nearer. If you are on the wrong road, progress means doing an about-turn and walking back to the right road; and in that case the [person] who turns back soonest is the most progressive. We have all seen this when doing arithmetic. When I have started a sum the wrong way, the sooner I

> admit this and go back and start again, the faster I shall get on. There is nothing progressive about being pig headed and refusing to admit a mistake. ... [If] we are on the wrong road, ... we must go back. Going back is the quickest way on."[4]

In my quest to understand how I could have made such a glaring error in my puzzle, I followed Lewis's advice and took a step back to evaluate the situation. The puzzle had 11 differently shaped pieces, but of those pieces, each one was duplicated in exactly the same size. This meant the entire puzzle required more frequent visits to the picture on the box to make certain they were in the right place. It required more time and "Fact Checking," if you will, with the original picture.

So, what did I learn?

Answer: even if a puzzle piece fits, it may be in the wrong place.

> **Even if a piece fits, it may be in the wrong place.**

That certainly was a revelation! The pieces did fit, but they did *not* match the picture on the box. Wow! I had never run into such a dilemma before. The trees looked just like the picture, but they were too high, so this section had to be completely *undone*. I then had to *rework* the puzzle in a variety of ways *until* I got it *just right*.

To accomplish this, I had to rely more heavily on colors because the shape itself was apt to be misleading. I can't tell you how many times I had to *undo* and *redo* multiple sections to finally get it right. The sky, the foreground,

---

[4] Lewis, C.S. (2001). *Mere Christianity*. San Francisco, CA: HarperCollins. Pages 28-29.

the vegetation and flowers, all tried and tested me and it didn't come together quickly or easily. But because I genuinely liked the picture on the box and was willing to pay the price to complete it, I persevered until I had fixed all of my mistakes and every piece was in its proper place.

It feels really good to accomplish something that is complicated and difficult. It is a feeling that can only come *after* paying the price in time, dedication, and perseverance to *get things right*. In real life, the stakes are often much higher than when assembling a puzzle. As such, you may have to pay even steeper prices in "blood, toil, tears, and sweat," as Winston Churchill once put it in one of his famous wartime speeches.

As I watch the rising generation grow up, I fear too many parents are not giving their children challenges and opportunities to sufficiently test and try them to the extent required to forge authentic character, integrity, self-discipline, and inner confidence. For there is a weathering process that can only occur in the midst of authentic trials and difficulties. There is no other way; you cannot buy experience or character at a store or order it for delivery on Amazon.com. True success comes from personal effort that is won the old-fashioned way: by paying the full price—not by having it handed to you.

Putting together challenging puzzles of a thousand pieces or more has reinforced important life lessons I have learned throughout my 77 years on the planet. These lessons include the following:

1. **I can do hard things.**
2. **If something is worth doing, then do it well—or not at all.**
3. **Things of value take time and effort to accomplish. You have to endure and pay the price to receive the rewards.**
4. **Where possible, avoid restricting yourself to a specific time frame to complete a difficult puzzle (or life challenge).**
5. **I am less likely to become discouraged and give up if I am passionate about what I am doing.**

The day after I finally completed the difficult *Tuscan Courtyard* puzzle, one of my neighbors came over to visit. I was delighted to show her my completed masterpiece. She looked at it for some time and then remarked, "Are you sure you got the beige and tan foreground right?" It seemed right to me, but after my friend left, I took a closer look at that section of the puzzle and realized she was right: it wasn't precise.

This realization presented me with a dilemma. Could I just leave it as it was? After all, most people would never see the picture on the box to compare, so why bother? This is a reasonable question to ask oneself, and there is more than one reasonable answer to it. However, because I *desired* precision in my work, I felt compelled to *undo* and then *redo* as many pieces as it took to get it exactly right. And in the end, I'm glad I did.

In life, there are times when we might be able to "cut corners" and otherwise produce subpar work without incurring external consequences. The problem with that approach is that I know the truth, and I feel better about myself and find my character fortified when I commit to traveling the extra miles required to achieve accuracy and precision.

Another lesson I learned from this experience is: a *second pair of eyes often sees what we don't*.

A Second Pair of Eyes often Sees what We Don't.

Sometimes we are *too close* to whatever we are working on to see things others might spot from a different (or more distant) vantage point. Applying a new perspective through someone else's eyes can help you see something you might have missed. So don't be afraid to ask for help or input from another person, and be willing to accept feedback and critiques which can improve the final result. Another perspective can always bless our efforts. Regardless whether the feedback is positive, constructive, or perhaps even critical, we can benefit from other perspectives if we are willing to be humble and teachable.

Doing so enriches our own capabilities and expands the possibilities of the end result.

So, how exactly do these lessons I've learned about puzzles relate to real life? Let's consider some examples…

Example One

I have a certificate in Interior Design. In the process of earning that accreditation, I discovered I have a good eye for colors, textures, shapes, and balance, all of which enhance my ability to create *"Feng Shui."* Feng shui is an Asian term used to describe the balance and harmony created as various elements such as colors, shapes, and objects are properly placed in a setting.

As an Interior Decorator, I can testify that the most common mistake homeowners make in hanging pictures is to hang them too high, especially if the ceiling is higher than usual. The picture or pictures may be in complete harmony with the colors and theme (e.g. Modern, Western, Italian, etc.) of the room; but if wrongly hung, it will detract from the room's *feng shui* (aka: the peace and harmony of the room). While untrained eyes may not see or understand the decorating principals involved, most will still be able to tell something is "off."

Most people aren't fully aware of how a decorative arrangement that lacks feng shui can influence one to feel nervous, uncomfortable, restless, or even tired. Even slight alterations to surrounding decor serves to restore *feng shui*, which can in-turn influence positive emotional states in those who frequent the space.

The Parthenon, built on the Acropolis in Greece, is touted to be the most perfectly designed building ever built. It is constructed according to the Aristotelian principle known as "The Golden Mean," which encompasses the following characteristics.

- **A middle ground between two extremes**
- **A desirable balance and harmony**

- **An attribute of beauty**
- **Not in excess............in other words, *feng shui***
- **Includes a two-third (2/3) to one-third (1/3) ratio.**

Aristotle's principle of the Golden Mean is another way of describing the concept of *feng shui*. Your life will be more productive and enjoyable if you incorporate harmonious balance (aka: *feng shui*) into your life, career, home, yard, and relationships.

Example Two

As a manager at a women's clothing store, it was my responsibility to help customers find clothing that fit and complimented their style, physique, hair color, skin tone, energy level, etc. After trying on an outfit, a woman would typically say to me, "Well, what do you think?" I always tried to be completely honest in my answer because I wasn't just selling an outfit; I truly wanted each woman to look fantastic.

This authenticity and integrity helped me earn the trust of my customers, which helped me (and the store) earn their business as repeat customers in the future. My goal was to create *feng shui* between a given outfit and the shopper at hand, so when a customer would ask me what I thought of a given outfit, I would reply with something like this, "The style and fit are perfect, but I don't think it's your best color." We would then shop together to find a color that better matched her hair, skin color, etc.

There are many situations in life where things may appear to "fit"; but that does not mean they are "just right." At this point, stop reading for a second and reflect on some of your own experiences where this was true for you, whether in a store, at work, in a personal relationship, or something else entirely. What did you do (or not do) about it? What might you have done differently if you could return to that place in your life or career with the experience and wisdom you have now?

One of the beautiful things about life is that as we age and gain experience and wisdom, we can get better at identifying and resolving our problems. It feels good to gradually grow into a "veteran" who is refined and polished at what you say or do. Such a status makes you knowledgeable, experienced, seasoned, trusted, and respected by others.

One of the things I will carefully examine in future puzzles, not to mention in my daily life, is to pay closer attention to details. This includes being aware of tasks at hand, my surroundings, what I have to work with, what my goal is, and how to plan and then execute that plan to create a positive end result—which is another way of saying: *getting it* RIGHT!

If we are willing to be good students, our life experiences can be great teachers. If we are willing to learn from the past, we will be willing to take measures to avoid past mistakes. Challenges manifest themselves as "ups and downs" with inherent consequences and results—depending on our choices. Getting something "Right" requires that we make correct choices along the way. Sometimes we make really lousy or even downright rotten choices, but that doesn't mean we can't *choose* to change our course and chart a better journey in the future.

Such is the ongoing hope of life!

Chapter 6
COMMITMENT & CONSISTENCY

This chapter discusses, among other things, the importance of commitment and consistency to completing a puzzle—or accomplishing any other worthy task, goal, or objective.

It was Christmas 2022. Many of my family and friends knew I thrived on assembling puzzles and that I was writing a book on how puzzling possessed parallels—both simple and complex—to our lives. Well, you probably won't be surprised to learn that several of my Christmas gifts were new puzzles!

I was particularly drawn to one called "Worlds Without End," which features Jesus Christ surveying his endless creations scattered across the heavens (outer space).

It reminded me of a puzzle of Mary and Baby Jesus I assembled a year earlier (*see* Appendix). It has lots of dark pieces which severely tested my patience and commitment to follow through. Gladly, I did see it through to completion. What bolstered my commitment and consistency when I ran into emotions of frustration and discouragement assembling all those dark pieces?

I think what helped a lot is that the subject of the puzzle really spoke to me, stirring a sort of motivational pathos in my soul as I worked. I felt connected to it spiritually—and that association fueled my consistence and

Worlds Without End puzzle box

commitment to complete it. After it was finished, I was pleased enough with the end result that I decided to Mod Podge and frame it.

I know the difference between ordinary puzzles and puzzles that really speak to me because I feel a desire to not only complete them, but also to make the images permanent and displayable by Mod Podging and then framing them. The greater the connection I feel to the puzzle, the more likely I am to push through the hard times and get it done, come what may. This experience taught me that the emotional and spiritual connection we feel (or don't feel) toward something we are doing plays a significant role in our ability to push through difficulties and finish the job. This is also true of the relationships we have with other people.

This new undertaking was a 500-piece puzzle, which I prefer to 1000-or-more piece puzzles. I like 500-piece puzzles in part because the tables in my home can better accommodate smaller puzzles of 500-pieces or less. Although this puzzle only had 500 pieces, I knew it wouldn't be an easy task.

If you desire to complete any puzzle—or life undertaking—you must be sincerely committed to it or you will most likely fail to follow through. If you lack a genuine interest and commitment to a puzzle—or anything else you attempt—your efforts may lead to discouragement, depression, and a lack of fulfillment. You may also end up viewing yourself as a failure, and perhaps even invite the derision and criticism of others, which may further deflate your sense of self-esteem and individual worth. Thus, how you feel about something *matters* because it will influence your thoughts and behavior throughout the process as well as contribute to the end result (or lack thereof).

If you don't like a given puzzle, search for one you do feel passionate about and begin your work there. If you love your choice of puzzle, you will enjoy the process of putting it together more than if you don't. Life is too short to be miserable; sometime "NO" is the best choice in both puzzling and in life. Choose to avoid misery by letting go of activities and relationships that exert negative influences over you.

Some puzzles I've undertaken did not bring me joy. As I looked at the incomplete picture coming into focus, I realized I wasn't enjoying the picture or the process, so why continue? Saying "no" does not always mean you are "quitting." It means you are pondering, evaluating, reassessing, and then choosing to let go of something in order to embrace something else that is better.

This topic reminds me of an experience I had 20 years ago in *Polly's Parlor*—my little gift shop in Southern Utah. In 2003, I decided to file for divorce from my husband of 36 years. I intended to move to Colorado after the divorce was finalized. In preparation for this move, I advertised everything in my store at a 30% discount to begin liquidating my inventory in preparation to close my shop prior to moving. A friend of mine in the community, who was a Catholic Priest, came in to my shop and asked me why the entire store was discounted. I told him that after 7 children and 36 years of marriage, I was filing for divorce, closing my shop, and leaving town for good. His response shocked and stunned me. Said he: "So you're quitting and giving up?"

With little hesitation, I quickly responded, "NO, I'm not a quitter. I've given my all and made a thoughtful and prayerful decision to leave my marriage for my long-term health, happiness, and well-being." Anyone who knows me and my situation and heart in the matter knows that I did not "quit" my marriage. After carefully analyzing all of the facts—and spending a decade trying my best to make things work—I made a calculated decision to end that particular relationship and move forward with my life in a different direction.

My fifth son, Jordan, introduced me to the following quote, which is often attributed to Albert Einstein: *Insanity is doing the same things over and over again and expecting different results.*

> "Insanity is doing the same things over and over again and expecting different results."
>
> Albert Einstein

When you have given your all to something or someone and negative results persist, it's time to evaluate and consider looking at other options, including choosing a new direction and course.

One of the most basic, yet vital, lessons we ever learn in our lives is that we can't change the behavior of another person any more than we can change the structure, piece size, piece number, or colors involved in a puzzle. It is perhaps one of the earliest lessons we all discover; yet it is probably one of the later lessons that we fully internalize and accept. While we can influence others, we can never control them—nor would we want to. After all, personal freedom is one of the greatest gifts in life. In the words of a great spiritual leader of the twentieth century, "*Next to the bestowal of life itself, the right to direct that life is God's greatest gift to man*[kind]."

> "Next to the bestowal of life itself, the right to direct that life is God's greatest gift to mankind."
>
> David O. McKay

Scripture teaches us that human beings were created for the purpose of obtaining JOY.[5] After more than three decades of marriage and endless efforts to make it work, it was time for me to accept the fact that certain things outside of my control had become "deal-breakers." The time had come for me to exercise the courage and discipline to do something about it. Part of this process involved recognizing my own weaknesses and limitations and being honest about the areas in which I had brought pain, sorrow, and difficulties on myself. Once I had arrived at this place, I could then make different decisions that could lead to better results in the future.

We are all human and will make incorrect decisions from time-to-time. But we can make restitution for our errors and choose a different pathway when we take responsibility for our mistakes and commit to attitudinal and behavioral changes. We do not have the power to alter the past; but we do have the power to change the present and thereby shape a better future for ourselves and those we love.

It really comes down to our individual choices.

It's up to ME *for* me. And it's up to YOU *for* you.

Now, back to my "World's Without End" puzzle. I already knew from previous experiences that puzzles with a lot of dark pieces are always challenging. Since this puzzle consisted of about 75% dark pieces, I debated whether to embark upon this particular puzzle at all. However, I had tackled other

---

[5] 2 Nephi 2:25, *The Book of Mormon*

puzzles in the past that came with similar difficulties. This fact boosted my confidence that I could invest the necessary commitment and consistence required to see the undertaking through to fruition, despite the difficulties involved.

One of my favorite movies is called *Shenandoah*, starring Jimmy Stewart. The story is set in the Southern United States during the American Civil War. Stewart plays a father with several sons. He becomes distressed when his youngest son—only 16 years old—leaves home to fight for the Confederacy. Distraught over his son's decision, Stewart's character decides to leave home in search of the boy. One of his older sons tries to convince him that the journey would be futile because they have no idea where to start, or where the boy might be, not to mention if he was still even alive.

I was only 15 years old when I first saw this movie and I'll never forget the father's reply to his older son. He said: *If we don't try, we don't do, and if we don't do, then why are we here?"*

> "If we don't *try*, we don't *do*, and if we don't *do*, then why are we here?"

What you *know* and *understand* are small things compared to what you actually *do* in your life. Furthermore, whether you like it or not and whether you know it or not, your actions do have an impact and influence on others, so it behooves us to try our best to be a positive and uplifting example to those around us.

We've all made bad decisions in our lives. Some of us have even made disastrous errors that we alone cannot fix. But even in the latter case the world still keeps spinning and we have to decide what we are going to do *next*. Fortunately, the power to *choose* is always in our hands. If we are willing to own up to our errors, fix the damage they caused (insofar as possible), and change course moving forward, we can still have a happy ending. It's not the end of the world to make a mistake—even a very big mistake. After all, some of the greatest human beings who have ever lived have made some epic mistakes in their lives. Some of them demonstrated through their actions that we each have the POWER to right our ship over time and get our life sailing successfully once again—even if we may have gotten *way off course*. What's more, others will observe your example and take inspiration from it. As such, don't ever underestimate the power of YOUR Example.

> **Never underestimate the Power of Your Example.**

In scripture, God gives us council and a clear path to pursue that, when followed, will bring us great JOY. I know this is true because I have experienced great joy when I've made correct decisions. On the flipside, I have also experienced great pain from making incorrect decisions.

Perhaps you don't believe in God or a higher power. That's okay. One of the greatest things about God is that He grants all of us free will to believe (or not believe) as our conscience directs. He further gives us freedom to choose what we will think about, say, and do.

On the other hand, what have you got to lose to investigate the possibility that there is a power greater than yourself that can actually help you along your journey? Divine intervention can minimize or even heal wounds of the heart, mind, and spirit that we inevitably incur along the way. It can save you from those dark places we sometimes find ourselves mired in. At least that has been my experience on many occasions throughout my life. As such, I invite you to put this phenomenon to the test. If you find that you are miserable at every turn, and nothing you've done thus far has seemed to help much, why not "draw upon that Higher Power" as Dr. Norman Vincent Peale suggested in his famous book *The Power of Positive Thinking*.

You didn't know how to ride a bike or swim when you were born, but you eventually learned. You didn't know how to read until someone taught you letters and phonics. You didn't know how to drive until you were instructed and then actually practiced operating a car. Everything you perform proficiently today was once a foreign concept and activity to/for you.

So why not give faith a try?

Unlike a puzzle—where we start out knowing *exactly* what our work will look like when we are done—real life requires a lot of faith to push through successfully; we don't have the end picture always before us as we go about our lives day-by-day. But this is not necessarily a bad thing. Because we cannot always see the end from the beginning in life, we have the opportunity to become an architect of our own lives. As the famous American poet, Henry Wadsworth Longfellow, wrote in his poem, *The Builders*:

> ALL are architects of Fate,
> Working in these walls of Time; ...
>
> For the structure that we raise,
>   Time is with materials filled;
> Our to-days and yesterdays
>   Are the blocks with which we build. ...
>
> Let us do our work as well,
>   Both the unseen and the seen;
> Make the house where Gods may dwell,
>   Beautiful, entire, and clean. ...
>
> Build to-day, then, strong and sure,
>   With a firm and amble base;
> And ascending and secure
>   Shall to-morrow find its place.

It is exciting to think that we can play a prominent role in the design and creation of our own life's story.

On the other hand, we must always remember that no matter how brilliantly, cleverly, or masterfully we try to design and orchestrate our plans, unforeseen events and challenges will arise. In other words, despite our best laid-out plans, *Life Happens*!

What exactly does that mean, *Life Happens*?

It means that we cannot control all of the variables all of the time. Consequently, unexpected trials and other events will compete with even your best-laid plans. At times, such adversity can be destructive and heartbreaking; but that doesn't mean your story is over. As someone once said: *Things will work out in the end. If they haven't worked out yet, it isn't the end!*

> "Things will work out in the end.
> If they haven't worked out yet, it isn't the end."[6]

This statement gives me hope. In fact, if there is one lesson that both life and puzzling have taught me again-and-again, it is *this*: come what may, there is always a reason to HOPE!

Below are a few of the endless variables that can alter, set back, or destroy your carefully designed conceptions of and/or plans for your life. These things can wreak havoc with your personal plans and blueprints.

- **Economic downturn or unexpected job loss**
- **Death of a loved one**
- **Accidents**
- **Weather**
- **Choices of others that negatively impact you beyond your control**
- **Physical, mental, and/or emotional heath crises beyond your control**

---

[6] Attributed to Tracy McMillan

My brother, Hyrum Wayne Smith, is just two years older than I am. This proximity in age led, in part, to our being very close friends growing up. Hyrum died in 2019 at age 76 from pancreatic cancer. Of all the cancer diagnoses one can receive, pancreatic cancer is one of the most lethal, and those who receive this diagnosis usually don't live long, leaving loved ones in shock. It was certainly a blow to me when I heard that my dear brother—only two years older than me—had only a few months to live. A seemingly healthy, energetic, and vibrant man doomed to die on a seeming dime! It was difficult news for me to take and process. A gifted and successful author, speaker, and business leader, Hyrum had touched the lives of millions. He had such a gift for positively influencing the lives of others. How could he be taken at such a relatively young age—and so suddenly! I couldn't imagine him gone from my life.

But guess what?

Life happens!

Hyrum died the same year he was diagnosed and there was nothing I could do about it. Moving forward, I had two choices. I could remain psychologically crippled and angry as I held on to the shock and pain of his passing. Or, I could move on by holding fast to all the good times and wonderful memories we forged together while growing up in Hawaii and New York.

The death of a loved one is a hard thing and appropriate mourning—which for me includes the shedding of many tears—is expected and okay. Such emotional states and experiences are part of the healing process. But allowing myself to be permanently damaged or crippled by Hyrum's death was not an option for me. It was Hyrum, in fact, who taught me this.

When Hyrum daughter and granddaughter were killed in a car accident more than 20 years earlier, I remember his speech at the funeral. Amidst his own palpable grief, it was he who was encouraging all present to hold on to the good memories and move forward with strength and courage. That was what I must do now.

I realized I now had the opportunity and responsibility to share with others the things Hyrum had taught me. They have blessed my life, so why not allow these things to bless others' lives as well? I know that is what he would want.

I'll never forget the day I received the news of Hyrum's cancer diagnosis. On a conference call with me and another brother, he explained to us in his regular, cheerful, and happy voice: *"Well guys, I wanted to tell you personally—before you get the word second hand—that I was just diagnosed with stage 4 pancreatic cancer and given two-to-four months to live, so pretty soon I'm going to be in a better place than you guys!"*

This was typical of Hyrum's sense of humor, but in this case, I was not amused! I chuckled, but said, *"Hyrum, that isn't funny!"* He replied: *"No it's not funny, but it's the truth."* You could have smacked me over the head with a two-by-four and I would not have been any less stunned. As the few months he had left slowly passed by, he remained upbeat and positive about his situation, making the most of every minute that remained. A man of great faith, he firmly believed he was heading to a better place—a belief I enthusiastically share.

In November, I got a phone call telling me he had passed away. Fortunately, my daughter Jessie happened to be staying with me for a few days, and I was grateful I wasn't alone when I received the news.

Hyrum wrote ten books. One of them was entitled: *What Matters Most: The Power of Living Your Values*. Another one was called: *Pain is Inevitable: Misery is Optional*. These books definitely helped me through some pretty tough times, and I knew that I would eventually heal from the pain of his passing.

Life changes for us on a daily basis. It regularly brings to us both big and small shifts we neither ask for, anticipate, nor expect. In many regards, we have no idea how our lives will progress or end. The hard work you invest towards your dreams and goals are important and generally deliver valued and well-deserved rewards, but there will always be unexpected events that alter or challenge even the best-made plans and dreams. Learning and accepting this reality will help us to "Go with the Flow" and avoid unnecessary additional suffering.

When I was growing up in Hawaii, did I have a plan or even an inkling that one day I would open a little gift shop called *Polly's Parlor* in rural Utah? No, I did not! Our lives tend to unfold in ways we never dreamed of, but it's always an exciting journey if we choose to perpetually see our proverbial "glass" as being "half-full" rather than "half-empty"—something else Hyrum taught me. Seeing the glass half full has been a blessing to me because I don't let unusual or unexpected life challenges and glitches take me hostage.

As a little girl, my ultimate goal was always to be a wife and mother. As a youth, I had only a tiny peek into what that mammoth process would entail. After going through 18 hours of labor for the birth of my first child—an 8-pound, 9-ounce son we named Paul—I realized my life would never be the same again. That experience produced the most agonizing physical pain I had ever endured, and made me think twice about my childhood ambition of bearing and raising twelve sons!

When Paul was just two years old, I was pregnant again, only this time I got much bigger than I did with the first pregnancy. A woman in town who had delivered nine children of her own assured me that you are always bigger with the second pregnancy. OK, that gave me a little peace of mind. Meanwhile, my doctor, without telling me what his stethoscope had revealed, sent mé off to get an x-ray. The baby was due on the 21st of June and he would be in New York for a medical convention. That meant another doctor might need to be alerted to deliver my child. An x-ray would be helpful in determining the actual time of birth. What he didn't tell me, however, was that he thought he heard two heart beats. Would you believe that I was expecting twins? Holy Smokes! I was going to have twins and my first child was only two! I was in a state of shock. Talk about unexpected news that was certainly not planned. So many things would change. First and foremost, I had to buy another crib—and trust me… that was the easiest part!

Did I ask for twins?

No!

Was I exhausted?

Yes, Yes, and YES!

I used to think I was tired during finals week at college. But I can testify that finals' fatigue doesn't hold a candle to the sleep deprivation I suffered after my twins were born. Nursing a baby every two hours of the day 24/7 produces a kind of debility that is indescribable. In fact, I recall once saying to my husband, "If an enemy comes for information and they threaten me with sleep deprivation as torture, I'll simply say: 'okay, what do you want to know?'"

My twin boys were born on May 29, 1970, three weeks prior to their due date of June 21st. We named them David and Wayne. Having three children in two-and-a-half years was not part of my original plan and required a new mindset to successfully handle. Then, to add to this difficulty, I gave birth to a fourth son, Joseph, one month after my oldest son turned four (4)—when my twins were only 19 months old! Your life circumstances and experiences will be different from mine, but the point is: expect the unexpected to weave its way into your life and trust in your capacity to handle whatever life throws at you as long as you are committed to doing the best you can.

I learned this principle from my mother, who was kind enough to come and spend two months at our home to help out with the twins after they were born. Even with her help I still felt exhausted and overwhelmed. Her home was 300 miles away from us at the time and I was not looking forward to having her leave. As she was about to depart, I felt deeply apprehensive and was on the verge of tears. Sensing my feelings and empathetic to my plight, she looked at me and said something I'll never forget: "*Young lady, just remember that God doesn't give you anything you can't handle.*"

> **"God doesn't give you anything you can't handle."**
>
> Mother

I believed her, and this faith helped get me through this incredibly challenging period of my life. I didn't ask for twins, but if God thought I could handle two babies along with a two-year old, then by golly I was not going to let God down! Today, my twin boys are in their mid-50s and empty nesters themselves! They and their wives brought me seven beautiful grandchildren between the four of them.

Let's take a look at one more example before I dive back into the *Worlds Without End* puzzle. Years ago, while completing my bachelor's degree in elementary education, I found myself doing my student teaching in a first grade classroom in Orem, Utah. One day the teacher was gone and my co-student teacher and I were in charge. My partner was telling the first graders a story as they sat on the floor around her. One of the boys started acting up, completely disrupting the class. My university professor just happened to be in the room evaluating us as teachers. My partner, who was much younger than me, was having a difficult time keeping the other children focused while trying to get the obstreperous boy to cooperate. After a while, I reached the point where I couldn't take it any longer. In an attempt to rescue her from this little brat, I walked over to get the boy and take him out in the hall where he wouldn't be able to disrupt the class any further. He fought me every step of the way—yelling, kicking and being as obnoxious as he possibly could. This boy had never demonstrated this kind of behavior in all the weeks I had been at the school. I had no idea why he was behaving so badly, and did not know what to say or do. As I hauled him out the door, I realized I needed help, so in my mind I said a little prayer asking God to tell me what to do.

The boy's behavior continued to be unruly in the hallway. I paused, wishing I could just smack him one, then took a deep breath, calmed myself, and waited for the answer I needed to deal with the situation. Softly, these words came to my mind: "Ask him what the problem is." I did, and after making eye contact with me and calming down somewhat, he said, "I didn't take my medication today."

I was stunned. I had no idea there were children in school that took medication to prevent the kind of behavior I just witnessed. I was speechless long enough that the child further said, "But the school nurse has some of my medication." I thanked him for being forthright with me and walked him down the hall to the school nurse. She gave him the medication. I then shared my lunch with him in the classroom because he was still too rowdy to accompany the other students to the lunch room.

After about 40 minutes, the young boy had calmed down to the point we were all accustomed to seeing in class. I was so relieved to have resolved the situation. I had been clueless as to what to do and felt desperate, so I asked... and then I *listened*. And I learned the truth of the statement: "Ask and ye shall receive." I've never forgotten that day because the answer came so swiftly and I was given understanding and wisdom from that Higher Power to deal with the situation.

There are many times in life when you need another person's help with something. In those instances, you usually have to *ask* for help. But what about the times when you desperately need aid that no human can offer? In those instances, I have found that heavenly help is available if I ask in *humility* and *faith*. I encourage you to do the same. Again, what do you have to lose to *try* calling upon that Higher Power?

One of the most practical things my brother Hyrum would teach in his time management seminars is that we all have exactly the same amount of time (24 hours per day). None of us can manufacture or create more time. It's the same 24 hours a day for each and every one of us. What happens in our 24-hour allotment depends on our desires, preferences, choices, efforts, dedication, and endurance. In other words, we have the power to *choose* how we use our time and the way we will respond to others around us, and the ways in which we use our time and *respond* to the people around us plays a significant role in determining the quality of our lives. If someone is rude, unkind, or dishonest with you, it is human nature to respond reactively and negatively. But the truth is that we have the power to *choose* our responses—even in negative situations.

One day, after spending an hour-and-a-half of my time puzzling, yet only managing to place two puzzle pieces where they belonged, I took a picture of my progress to show what I had completed and what still needed to be done.

Worlds Without End in process

As you can see, the remaining pieces were very similar and dark in color, which made it extra challenging. What I had already assembled had proved difficult, and my progress pleased me greatly. Yet what remained would be similarly tricky and would require a determined investment of both effort and time—as the past 90 minutes of mostly failure had illustrated.

At this point the thought crossed my mind: why not Mod Podge it as is and call it something like "Unfinished," or "Miles to Go," or "God sees what we do not." I could easily write an entire chapter on this unfinished puzzle that could be entertaining, enlightening, and share some important points. But deep down, I really did want to complete this puzzle regardless of the difficulties involved. In my mind was a vision of what it would look liked finished, Mod Podged, and beautifully framed.

This vision spurred on my desire and determination to finish it. After investing many more hours of my time and wading through many frustrating moments, I got down to the last two pieces, only to discover that those two pieces were missing!

Worlds Without End Puzzle with two missing pieces

This seemed impossible because it was a brand new puzzle! I had opened it myself and was diligent about picking up all pieces that may have fallen onto the kitchen floor. I always check everything around the table to make sure I have all the pieces, just in case one fell and I didn't hear it. But try though I might, I could not locate the two missing pieces.

Ok, now what?

First of all, I didn't freak out because I have learned from past experience that panicking only exacerbates the situation. Instead, I was reminded of a phrase my mother always shared when I misplaced something and couldn't find it. It goes like this: "Backtrack through your mind." I put a lot of stock in this statement of hers because about 80 percent of the time I would find what I was looking for as long as I *backtracked through my mind.*

So, I said a little prayer, backtracked through my mind, and then went searching for those two missing pieces. After several days had gone by, however, the two pieces were still missing.

Now what should I do?

Fortunately, this had happened to me before when I was assembling a puzzle of the Founding Father's signing the Declaration of Independence. It was also a new puzzle and one piece was missing.

Instead of panicking, I evaluated my options. I could repurchase the same puzzle and search for the missing piece, or… I could make a homemade new piece and insert my own handiwork! I really wanted to complete this puzzle and the time and money required to purchase a duplicate and go searching through all the pieces looking for the ones I needed seemed not only costly and counterproductive, but not much fun either.

So, I set out to make a substitute puzzle piece from scratch. Creativity was of the essence, because the piece had to be as thin as the other pieces and the colors had to be accurate enough to appropriately blend with the surrounding pieces to avoid standing out as an obvious facsimile.

It was not easy, but after I had invested the necessary time, patience, and creativity, my final result yielded a highly satisfactory replacement!

Founding Fathers Puzzle with one missing piece

Worlds Without End completed

I knew I had done a good job when my brother came over for a visit and was unable to tell where the two substitute pieces were located.

As I looked at my completed puzzle, I felt a surge of satisfaction and fulfillment for having "Finished the Race," as the saying goes. After completion, I Mod Podged and framed this puzzle. It now hangs in my youngest daughter's new house (in their library) and serves as a wonderful asset to the overall ambiance of their lovely home.

This double success of having completed a difficult puzzle *and* adequately compensated for the two missing pieces built my self-esteem as a puzzler. And so it is in life. We all need to know that we are capable of doing hard things. We also need to remember that if our "Plan A" doesn't work out, we can tap into our creativity and ingenuity and formulate an innovative "Plan B" or "C." Knowing the puzzle was now whole and complete gave me a quiet reassurance that there is usually more than one way to accomplish a given task. I hope you will remember this the next time you find yourself *stuck* in the midst of a challenging project or undertaking. And if you are a parent, I further encourage you to teach and model these same principles and practices with your children by cheering them on as they work through their own obstacles and difficulties.

When my 7th child was 8-years old, my mother came for a visit. During her stay, I asked her if she had any regrets in her life. I'll never forget her response, which surprised me. She said: "No: I don't have any regrets because I did the best job I knew how to do at the time."

What a great answer!

And what a wonderful way to live!

Just think about that for a minute.... In the end, isn't that all that any of us can ever hope to accomplish: *the best we are capable of at any given moment in time?* None of us are perfect, and of course we all make mistakes. But there is hope in our potential to always do our best—however *imperfect* that may be at any given period of our lives. Glitches are an almost constant occurrence in our lives, meaning we have to continually evaluate, regroup, and decide on alternative plans—in other words: do our best in whatever circumstances we may find ourselves.

Interestingly enough, after I Mod Podged the puzzle with the two missing pieces, I ended up finding the original pieces. They were hiding at the bottom of the puzzle box, which I hadn't yet checked. I have no memory putting them there myself and it was a genuine mystery how they ended up there. My children were all grown and gone, so I knew I could not blame them.

So strange!

But then I remembered I had prayed to find those pieces, hopefully *before* I had already made their replacements. I've learned from experience that prayers are not always answered in the *way* or *time* we might think or expect, but I'm convinced finding them was an answer to my prayer. It reminds me of a saying my son, Jordan, once heard from a female religious leader he respected: "*God always answers prayers. Sometimes He says 'Yes' sometimes He says 'No' and sometimes He says 'Wait a while.'*" —Darlene Andrus

> "God always answers prayers. Sometimes He says 'Yes' sometimes He says 'No' and sometimes He says 'Wait a while.'"
>
> Darlene Andrus

Life will always throw you curveballs, but that is not necessarily a bad thing. I firmly believe that sometimes the *seeming* glitches are what actually make our lives better because adversity stretches, refines, and ultimately polishes you into a better and stronger individual. In the words of Thomas Carlyle: *Adversity is the diamond dust that heaven polishes her jewels with.*

> "Adversity is the diamond dust that heaven polishes her jewels with."
>
> Thomas Carlyle

Earlier in this book, I shared a couple of quotes from two plaques I have displayed in my kitchen. I think it is worth repeating these quotes here. One reads: *Let your Faith be Bigger than your Fears.* The other one reads: *You can do the Impossible because you have been through the unimaginable.*

> Let Your Faith be Bigger than your Fears.

> "You can do the impossible because you have been through the unimaginable."
>
> Christina Rasmussen

I appreciate the principles and truths contained in these two statements and read them every day of my life to help inspire me to be the best I can be. They provide continual comfort and guidance. They also help me remember to remain committed to what matters most to me and be consistent in doing what's right—the same principles that have helped me to become an effective and accomplished puzzler!

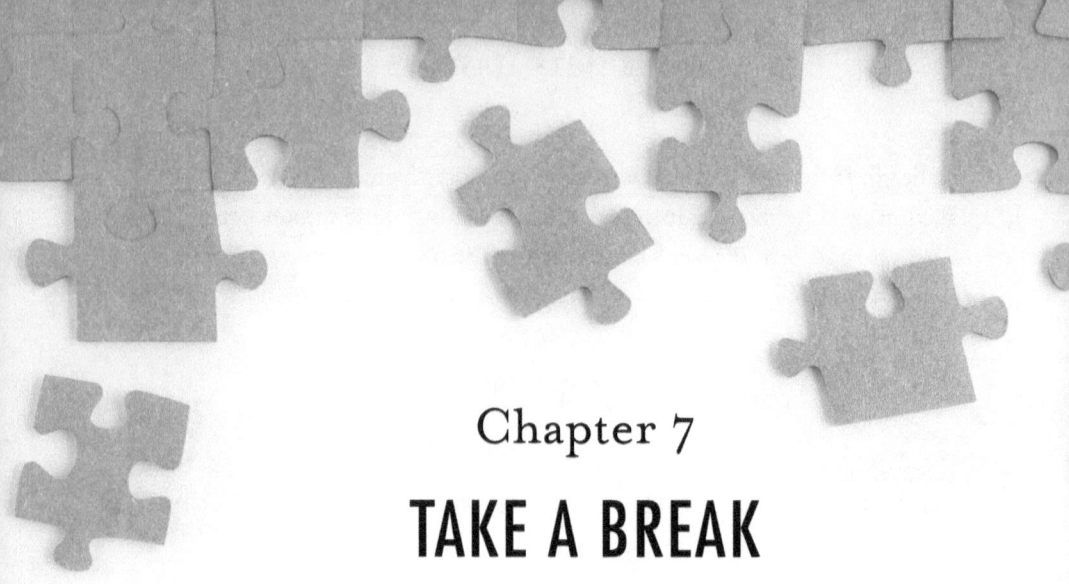

Chapter 7

TAKE A BREAK

We all face stress in our lives. It's part of the human condition and experience. Negative stress can serve as the underlying cause of multiple ailments and conditions, which, if unaddressed, can actually kill you!

That is the bad news about stress.

The good news is that all stress is not bad for you. Some stress can actually be a positive influence in your life because it can help spur you on to improve, excel, and otherwise motivate productive action and accomplishment. Psychologists refer to this kind of (positive) stress as *eustress*.

When I was 24 years old, I gave birth to twin sons when I already had a two-year old son at home. I was nursing a baby every two hours around the clock and quickly discovered how agonizing sleep deprivation can be. One night, I had just nursed one of the babies and collapsed back into bed when about 10 minutes later I heard crying and flew back into the nursery. One of my babies had just been fed and one was really hungry, but I didn't know which was which! How could this be? How could I possibly forget which baby I had just nursed? I thought I was tired during finals week in college, but this took fatigue to an entirely new level, and it was very stressful!

One of my favorite sayings is: *That which does not kill you makes you stronger.*

> "That which does not kill you makes you stronger."

I can attest to the truth of this statement. I definitely became a lot stronger raising three young boys under the age of two!

Two additional sayings I love are: A *change is as good as a rest*, and *all work and no play makes Jack a dull boy.*

> "A change is as good as a rest."
> Winston Churchill

> "All work and no play makes Jack a dull boy."

These maxims remind me of the importance of seasoning my life's experiences with balance and variety. My brother Hyrum Wayne Smith, a modern time management guru and motivational speaker taught that obtaining a positive, productive, and happy experience in this life boils down to four basic things:

1. **To live**
2. **To love and be loved**
3. **To feel important**
4. **To experience variety**

I have found this to be true in my own life and would like to focus on number four (4) *variety* in this chapter because one puzzle in particular reminded me just how important variety is in our lives. As the old saying goes: variety truly is the "Spice of Life!"

I had been working long hours and many days on a particularly difficult 500-piece puzzle. I was tired of working on the puzzle and my experiences have taught me that "Puzzle Block" can be as real as "Writer's Block." It was time to take a break and do something different.

When you are deeply engrossed in a puzzle, but failing to make much progress, I've learned it's time to step back, take a break, and evaluate things from a distance. Working on something you enjoy is much like eating *Fritos*, *Doritos*, or some other delectable treat you find addictive; it seems like you always have to have *just one more*. So it is with puzzles! As a result, I often feel compelled to put in just one more piece where it belongs before I stop. But if I'm not careful, I can end up turning into a quasi-zombie as "one more" turns into *another*, and then *another*, and then *another*. In other words, just like a prudent gambler knows when to say "enough" and walk away, you need to be able to recognize when it is time to "stop," take a break, and look at your work from a different perspective.

I've discovered that when I stand up and look at a puzzle from a distance, I see it not only in a different light and angle, but also in a different perspective which, in-turn, empowers me to move forward and achieve a breakthrough which had previously seemed inaccessible. If this technique doesn't help, it's time to take a complete break and do something else.

As I assessed the situation with my new puzzle, I determined I was at a place where I needed a complete break from the puzzle, so I decided to go outside and take a walk. Shortly after I had returned home, a neighbor knocked on my door. It was a dear friend. The purpose of her visit was to bring me a new puzzle she thought I would enjoy. It was in a sandwich zip lock bag, so I knew it was pretty small (I measured it upon completion and it was only 11 x 7 inches). After eating a bite of lunch, I was drawn to doing this little puzzle because I liked the picture of the little cottage, which was so "English." I love everything that makes me think of the British Isles, in part because that is where many of my ancestors originated.

English Cottage *by* Thomas Kincaid

Due to the diminutive size of the puzzle, it only took me 40 minutes to assemble. It wasn't complicated or challenging—just what I needed as part of my "break" from the larger, more difficult puzzle I had temporarily walked away from. Not only did I have a change of "scenery," but the satisfaction of completing a smaller project so quickly and effortlessly was fulfilling and energizing.

Whatever undertaking in which you are currently involved, recognize *when* you need to stop, step back, take a break, and get a new perspective on what you are doing. Sometimes a change of course is required, timely, and necessary for you to be able to make further progress. Other times, someone else's perspective may be the answer to your dilemma, so don't be too shy to look outside yourself for answers from those who might be able to see what you are missing.

Chapter 8
BE INFORMED

A maxim is a short, concise expression of wisdom—an elegant or poetic statement that expresses a general truth or rule of conduct. To give you an idea of some famous maxims, consider a few that I consider particularly noteworthy.

- To have what you want is riches, but to be able to do without is power.[7]
- Fear is the habit of anticipating the worst.
- Being witty is like being slim—it's beastly hard work.[8]
- Duty makes us do things well, but love makes us do them beautifully.[9]
- What you do speaks so loudly I cannot hear what you say.[10]
- I'm always home except when I'm not.

---

[7] George McDonald
[8] Clemence Dane
[9] Zig Ziglar
[10] Ralph Waldo Emerson

Just for the record, I concocted that last one myself. Sorry, I just couldn't resist the temptation to share it, as there never was a truer statement and I'm hopeful you got at least a small grin on your face when you read it. A statement which shares truth and simultaneously invokes laughter is what I call a double-whammy maxim, or stated more succinctly, a maxim*um*.

If a simple statement can positively, mentally and emotionally move someone and at the same time invoke laughter, the reader is doubly blessed. Despite being short and to the point, maxims are wonderful in their capacity for prompting us to ponder, reflect, and evaluate our lives within a context of their shared wisdom.

A dear friend shared with me the following maxim: *He who asks the questions controls the conversation.* An example of this is the gentleman who asks his friend: "Why is it you always answer a question with a question?" To which his friend replied: "Why not?"

And with that pithy diversion, let's get back to puzzles…

Before purchasing and then starting a puzzle you need to know certain facts. Below is a simple, but important list.

1. How many pieces are in the puzzle?
2. What size are the individual pieces?
3. Do the pieces come in a variety of shapes, or are they all the same?
4. Is your selected surface area (table) big enough to handle this number of pieces?
5. Are the colors concentrated or dispersed?
6. Are the shades of color darker, lighter, both, or a spectrum?
7. What is my purpose in doing this puzzle?
8. What are my time allotments or restrictions?

Chances are you would not ask yourself these questions on your first go-round. But after assembling scores of puzzles, I have learned that asking and then answering these questions helps to simplify the puzzling process. Knowing the answers to these questions will help you more fully enjoy your puzzling experience. Remember that scripture teaches we were created so we might have joy.[11] Answering these questions will help limit stress and stumbling blocks to the puzzling process and increase your joy in the journey. I have also discovered that recruiting someone to help you assemble a puzzle is an added bonus because working together on such a project lends itself to good conversation.

Perhaps you have never enjoyed assembling puzzles. If this is the case, I encourage you to ask yourself "why"? I suspect there are some individuals who genuinely do not enjoy puzzling, and that is okay. However, I believe there are usually reasons for this dislike that could be overcome. For example, one reason for not enjoying puzzling may stem from an initial introduction to the activity that proved too difficult, or involved a picture that was uninteresting to you. If this has been your experience, I hope reading this book will encourage you to give puzzling another shot with a puzzle that is both interesting and doable.

If you are willing to give puzzles another chance, I know you can discover—as I have—that puzzling is more than just a game or an entertaining way to pass time on a rainy day (or during a pandemic). It has the potential to give you greater vision and understanding of things you face in real life… every single day.

To help in this process, I encourage you before starting a puzzle to ask yourself the question: "What will this puzzle teach me?" or "What might I learn from tackling this challenge?" In other words, intentionally look for and seek what can be taught and learned as you proceed to puzzle. Then dive in and enjoy!

Education comes in many forms. It is not exclusive to formal schooling provided in schools or institutions of higher education. I assume that most of us—most of the time—are learning new things every day of our lives. If not, perhaps we need to pay closer attention to what life is trying to teach us.

---

[11] 2 Nephi 2:25, *The Book of Mormon*

Not a day passes in my life when I don't learn something new, and this fact makes life exciting, adventurous, and variety-filled. Like it or not, all kinds of things happen in our lives every day. The trick is to sift through our experiences and discover the life lessons as they arise. From the great wartime leader, Winston Churchill, we learn that: "a leader is often his [or her] *own* best teacher."[12]

> "A leader is often his [or her] own best teacher."
>
> Winston Churchill

If we are always waiting for someone else to teach us everything we know, we will miss out on countless learning opportunities from life itself—by virtue of careful observation, study, analysis, and scrutiny of our experiences. While life itself will not instruct us with the spoken word, our minds have the capacity to interpret our experiences in ways that are chock full of educational insights. If we are paying attention, we can learn so much from our own observations and intuition as a self-instructor. Furthermore, if we pay close attention and really listen, that Higher Power will teach us many things as well—at least that has been my experience.

Bearing and raising seven children provided me with an education I could have never gained in a formal classroom. Character traits such as: patience, fortitude, strength, resilience, and endurance (physically, mentally, and emotionally) can be taught in a classroom, but they must be developed in the laboratory of daily living. There is no other way. And it is *character*—even more than education alone—that is needed to succeed in life.

---

[12] Mansfield, Stephen (1995). *Never Give In: The Extraordinary Character of Winston Churchill*. Nashville, TN: Cumberland House Publishing Inc. Page 227.

> "We must remember that intelligence is not enough. Intelligence plus character—that is the goal of true education."
>
> Dr. Martin Luther King, Jr.

Parents have the privilege of being able to teach and model this reality in hopes of equipping their children with both the education and character they need to succeed in the real world.

But remember: parents eventually pass on. If they have not given their children the tools necessary to do well in life, they will have seriously stifled their progeny's possibilities. Second only to ensuring a child's shelter, safety, and basic nourishment, a parent's duty is to teach and develop character—for it is character that will ensure the child's long-term success and prove a net asset to society-at-large. There is no greater gift than the privilege of guiding a child and otherwise helping him or her to reach one's best and highest potential. This, in-turn, is the greatest gift you can bestow on a child. And along the way, there is no greater satisfaction and joy than succeeding in this ongoing process of character development.

As you influence others—including your children—for good, they will in-turn enrich and empower others as well. You never know how far-reaching these rippling effects can travel. Always remember that YOU have more strength than you realize and that spreading positivity and joy invites a full measure of the same to return to you, with interest! Never forget the words from *Shenandoah*: "If we don't try, then we don't do; and if we don't do, then why are we here?"

> "If we don't try, then we don't do; and if we don't do, then why are we here?"
>
> From the movie, *Shenandoah*

I confess that when I first started puzzling, I didn't gather much information about a puzzle before I started. But the more puzzling I did, the more I realized how different each puzzle was and therefore began to develop different strategies for undertaking each one.

For example, I've found that it is sometimes more effective and productive to sort pieces according to their shape as well as their color before diving right in and working more randomly. We can learn a lot from trial-and-error—about puzzling and life.

There is a saying my mother used to say to me and it went like this: *The first time it's the dog's fault; the second time it's YOURS.*

> "The first time it's the *dog's* fault; the second time it's YOURS."

This humorous maxim reminds us that while "to err is human," we also have a responsibility to learn from our mistakes in an effort to not continually repeat them. It's just as important to learn from your mistakes as it is to learn from your successes. In fact, it's probably even *more* important.

When puzzling, I am of the opinion—and most people would probably agree with me—that searching for and separating all the edge pieces is the best tactic to begin with. The reason for this is because the edge pieces form the framework and dimensions of the puzzle's boundaries. Once you are clear on the frame, you can focus on what comes within its borders. Of course, the size and dimensions are written on the box along with the picture, but sometimes I can clearly see that two opposite sides are not the same length, which tells me I've done something wrong. This is when my measuring tape comes in handy. When two opposite sides of your puzzle are either too short or too long, you need to figure out why. A measuring tape helps you get back on track. If your finished frame does not add up to the stated dimensions on the box, you know for sure an error has been made and you can begin to make the necessary adjustments.

Among my most challenging experiences as a puzzler occur when two pieces fit together *seemingly* perfectly, but as you progress you discover that just because it fits doesn't mean it is in the right place—and if it isn't right, other pieces will end up in the wrong place also. I dislike the game of trial-and-error that accompanies these "puzzles" within a puzzle. But it is a game I sometimes have to play in puzzling and in life.

Recently I tackled a difficult but inspiring puzzle. It is called I*n Green Pastures*, but I refer to it as *The Lost Lamb*. My second son, David, who is in his early 50s, came to visit and helped me start this puzzle.

In Green Pastures / The Lost Lamb nearing completion

David and Wayne (my twin sons) are puzzling masters, which is a real gift—and a big help to me whenever they are available to help out. But the best part of working with David or Wayne (or both) is the mother-son bonding time we enjoy together. On this particular puzzle, David worked exclusively on assembling the more obvious interior pieces while I tackled the edges. After two hours of combined effort, I had completed the edges and he had assembled Jesus, the lambs, and the outer sides of the tree trunk. The easy part was done!

The rest of the puzzle was nothing short of a nightmare. I thought finishing the tree would be a piece of cake because the brown pieces were so obvious compared to the rest of the picture. Boy was I wrong! Although it was clear that certain pieces were obviously part of the tree, I was stunned at how difficult it was finding where those pieces actually belonged. Years ago, I may not have persisted to complete this challenge. But my growing knowledge and experience gave me the confidence to push through the rough patches and get the job done.

In life we tend to navigate our responsibilities and opportunities similarly. We often choose the tasks that are quick and easy to master before going on to more difficult and time-consuming challenges. To illustrate this point, consider your current "To-Do List" at home or work. Typically, we will look the list over, isolate the tasks that take less time and effort and dive into getting them out of the way before engaging in tougher, more complicated and time-consuming assignments.

Why do we typically approach our "to-do" lists in this way? I think it is because as human beings we take great delight and satisfaction in checking off or crossing out a completed task and if you do two or three items right away you feel especially good about yourself, pat yourself on the back, and internally affirm something along the lines of: "Great Job; I am awesome!" As my brother Hyrum—the *Franklin Day Planner* guru—used to tell his time management seminar attendees: "Crossing off an item on a check list is like pure morphine." Furthermore, the list is now much shorter and *seemingly* less daunting that it was before because of your efforts. However, "AWESOME" often feels short lived as the day progresses and you run out of time to get to the more difficult tasks, which are usually much more important or urgent than the small and simple tasks you initially set out to do.

While there is nothing inherently wrong with starting with the easier tasks to gain that quick shot of adrenaline, we must not let that momentary victory distract us from the more important and urgent tasks on our lists. One way of avoiding this dilemma is to simply start off with the more difficult tasks and complete them first. This act of "delaying gratification" can be motivating because we are not only making progress on our list items that matter most, but know that we have the quicker, easier tasks awaiting us later on when we will likely have less time, energy, and motivation.

In Green Pastures / The Lost Lamb complete

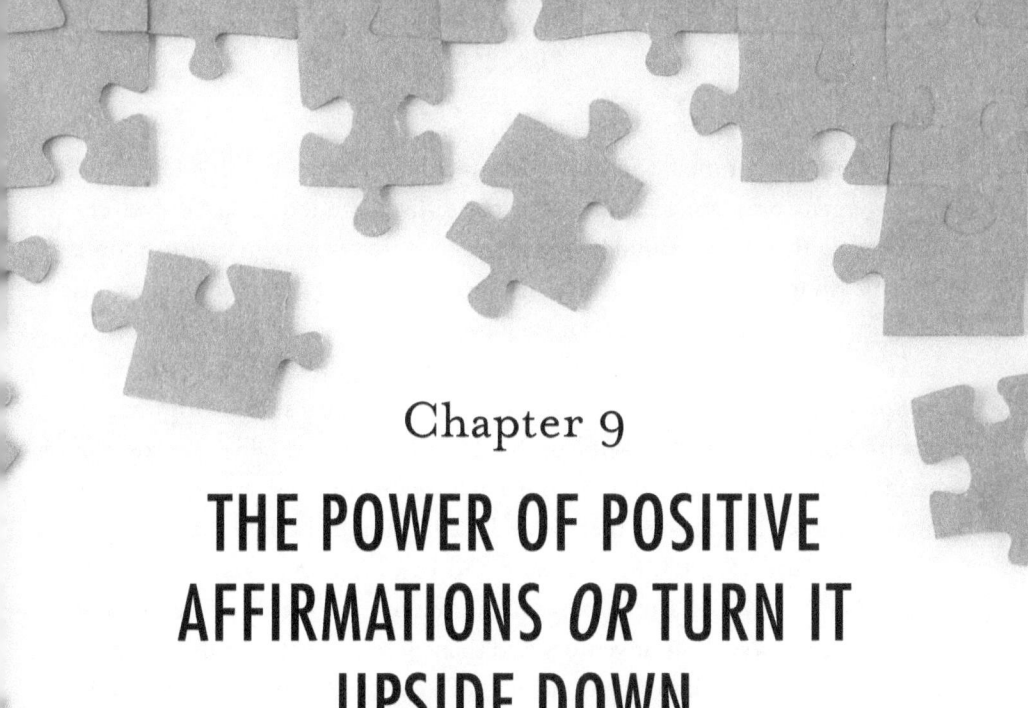

Chapter 9

THE POWER OF POSITIVE AFFIRMATIONS *OR* TURN IT UPSIDE DOWN

Do you know what an affirmation is?

An affirmation is a positive declaration written as a truth you believe in. It may also describe a specific behavior and outline a time frame for realizing an objective.

In my late 50s, I enrolled in the Starkey International Institute for Household Managers, which is sort of like the American version of English Butler training. We students referred to the school as "Butler Boot Camp" because like military boot camps, the training was demanding, draining, and could sometimes feel a little demeaning as they cut us down before building us back up.

During my training I was introduced to the concept of affirmations. I was required to write a positive affirmation for myself, which would be graded. No Stress there! As simple as this assignment might sound in theory, I was really struggling with it, not to mention the entire butler training program. I had recently been divorced and was not in a positive mindset. You might say I was an emotional wreck and my mental state made this Household Management program feel like the most difficult undertaking I'd ever encountered. That might sound like a strange thing to say in light of other, more difficult things I had already accomplished—such as raising seven (7) children, graduating from college, and achieving success as an *Avon* saleswoman and small business retail owner. Yet at *this* point in my life, this new challenge *seemed* tougher than all the rest. But why? I think it had to do with my lack of self-esteem at the time. Even Mrs. Starkey (the program Director) saw it in me and sent me to a trained professional who added to my stress by telling me I was depressed and needed therapy and medication. I suppose she was right.

It was April of 2003. My husband and I had separated and our divorce was looming. I was at a rock bottom and felt lower than dirt. I decided to liquidate my *Polly's Parlor* inventory and then close my little gift shop. I loved managing that little shop; it had helped me keep my sanity during the darkest days of my first marriage. I gave it up because I didn't want to live in the same town where my soon-to-be ex-husband resided. I was literally having to take up decade-old roots and start an entirely new life. My youngest child, Jessie, was graduating from college at the end of the summer. It was only 18 days after the death of my sister Lynne, to whom I was close. After 37 years of marriage, 7 children, and a dozen-or-so grandchildren (I have 31 now) my life was being turned upside down and I felt terrible. I was also leaving a large, beautiful two-story home that I helped to build nearly three decades earlier.

After I finished my studies at the Starkey School, I had no idea where I would go or what I would do. All of these variables made the program much harder than it would have been under less stressful circumstances. I was studying until midnight each day and still not totally caught up with all I'd been taught the day before. The material and instructors were extremely demanding and I was being immensely challenged physically, mentally, and emotionally.

Feeling beyond wretched as I did, how could I possibly come up with a great positive affirmation, which, to add to my stress, would be graded? To top things off, If I missed two days of classes, I would be kicked out of the program, which meant I could not attend my daughter Jessie's college graduation. Tuition to the Starkey School cost $13,000 and I couldn't afford to be kicked out.

Part of our training required that we wear uniforms every day. I found it very boring to look in the mirror and see the same-ole-me dressed the same-old-way day-after-day-after-day. After all, clothes do add a certain amount of variety and spice to life, which can brighten your day. In the midst of this very difficult period of time in my life, I constructed the following affirmation:

I am beautiful, elegant, smart, and do well in school. I am a good student and diligently study until I understand any material, but never study on Sundays.

Despite the challenges involved, I did graduate with a 93 percent average, and regularly repeating this affirmation helped! After all, when I looked in the mirror, it told me I looked stressed (*which I was*) not beautiful, and the uniform I wore every day looked okay, but definitely did not spell "elegant." However, I taped this affirmation to my mirror, and as instructed by Mrs. Starkey, said it out loud multiple times each day.

The Starkey School was located in Denver Colorado, where my oldest sister Ruth lived. If it were not for Ruth's generosity—which blessed the lives of me and my children on many occasions throughout our lives—I would not have survived as well as I did. Ruth was a financially well-to-do widow and influential member of her church and community. One weekend, she called and asked me to host a table at a fundraiser for the Denver Young Artists Orchestra (Ruth was on its Board of Directors). She had paid for two tables and invited guests to fill both, and since she couldn't be in two places at once, asked me to host the other table. Ask me if that was temping? However, I declined because I had already committed to study until midnight every night except Sunday and I felt that I could not afford to sacrifice an entire evening of study. But Ruth persisted by laying out a logical and credible defense of why I legitimately needed a break and explained how taking the night off would actually be good for me.

Her pitch was persuasive enough that I decided it wouldn't hurt too much to take the night off and attend. Such an occasion required fancy elegant attire, which I had, but it was at Ruth's house, as I only needed my uniform at school. So, she picked me up to take me to her house so I could get ready for the evening.

I will never forget the emotions that enveloped me as I "dressed to the nines" complete with feminine shoes and jewelry to compliment my elegant attire. I was blown away when I looked in the mirror. Was that really me? I'd forgotten what I looked like in something other than the same old uniform day-after-day and the sight of this transformation brought tears to my eyes. I genuinely did look beautiful *and* elegant, just as I had been repeating over-and-over in my affirmation. More importantly, I truly felt both elegant and beautiful—on the inside and out. There is no doubt I behaved beautifully and elegantly hosting Ruth's guests who were assigned to my table. It was a special evening and the food was delicious.

I am so glad Ruth convinced me to come!

As you might recall from a previous chapter, variety is not just important; it's essential! From the great wartime leader, Winston Churchill, we learn that "when a leader needs a break, a change is often as good as a rest."[13] I was a firm believer of *this* principle after *that* night. To escape from the Starkey Mansion, dress like a princess, and feel like a queen was food for my soul. At evening's end, I felt capable of surviving anything… or at least another week at school.

When I returned to the mansion that night, a fellow student-colleague of mine, a retired Marine named Mr. Champion (yes, that really was his name), who, in my estimation, looked like a Prince, was in the kitchen making a sandwich. Except for the day I arrived at the Starkey Manion, he had never seen me in anything but my prescribed uniform and certainly never dressed

---

[13] Mansfield, Stephen (1995). *Never Give In: The Extraordinary Character of Winston Churchill*. Nashville, TN: Cumberland House Publishing Inc. Page 227.

to the hilt the way I was when I walked into the kitchen at about 1:00 am. I'll never forget the way he looked at me and then said: "You look absolutely gorgeous."

It was a perfect ending to a perfect evening. I felt like Cinderella. Living in the Starkey Mansion as a student recruit had already made me feel like Cinderella, the overworked chambermaid—*before* she got her prince—but now I felt like Cinderella at the ball visiting with *the Prince*. The two of us had a lovely visit together in the living room of the Mansion. Afterward, he walked me up to my room, complimented me again on how beautiful I looked, and gently kissed me good night.

What a gentleman!

What a moment!

What a memory!

Now for me, that was a Cinderella story come true, and the kiss was the icing on the cake. You could never convince me that the affirmation I repeated multiple times a day had not had a profound effect on me and how I felt about myself, thus fueling my personal transformation that made this special evening possible. The movie, *The Devil Wears Prada*, tells a story similar to what I experienced at the Starkey School and I always cry when I watch it.

I know now from personal experience that affirmations work, and the more consistently you repeat them each day, the more effective they can be. If you have something in your life that you really want, or would like to see happen, I highly recommend writing your own affirmation. Then read it aloud every day without exception. Multiple recitations per day is even better. If you remain dedicated to this practice, the resulting power in your life is unexplainable, but real—and positive.

Writing a book can be a daunting prospect. It certainly was for me, and I experienced my share of "Writer's Block" along the way. It's tricky setting aside the time needed to write so much. It's also tricky organizing your thoughts into a coherent structure. Plus, as I've said several times now, *Life Happens!* With all of these challenges standing in between me and publishing this book, I reflected back on my time at the Starkey School, and realized it might help if I wrote another affirmation for myself. So, I did, and here is what it said:

I have a powerful message to share, and I am a great communicator and writer. I will complete my book by the middle of April 2023, giving my editor time to make sure my book will be in print, published, and in my hands by December 7th, 2023.

Once again, I placed this statement on a card where I would see it and could repeat it several times each day; and once again, it helped me to realize my objectives.

It's important to note that affirmations are useless if they are unrealistic or if you refuse to take any action on them. For example, in addition to repeating this affirmation each day, I also set a goal to spend two (2) hours each day *actually* writing. It's one thing to repeat an affirmation. It's quite another to spend two hours every day writing! But as I was faithful in repeating my affirmation *and* taking concrete action each day, my objective not only came into sharp focus, but was eventually realized. How do I know? Well, it has been said that the *proof is in the pudding*; and you are holding "the pudding" in your hands right now.

Mission Accomplished!
    Affirmation Achieved!!
        Vision Fulfilled!!!

If you have something in your life that you really want, or would like to see happen, I highly recommend you write yourself an affirmation, read it every day (or better yet, several times a day), set (and achieve) realistic goals along the way, and stick to your objective no matter what. If you will remain dedicated to this process, the power it will have in your life is not entirely explainable, but very real.

Perhaps you may be thinking, "Wait a minute, didn't she already say this several paragraphs back?" The answer is: "Yes," but I repeated it because I think it's worth saying twice. Nearly a century ago, my father—a professor of speech and drama—coauthored a book entitled: *The Fundamentals of Speech* wherein he taught that "repetition makes for learning."[14] Whether you are studying speech, affirmations, or something else, the idea that *Repetition leads to Reception* is a great educational truth. Again, in the words of my father: "The process must be by way of education in ideas, of fertilizing the thinking process, of enriching the imagination, the memory, and one's store of facts. On top of all must come drill and criticism, practice and analysis, observation, study, and much repetition."[15]

Don't ever underestimate the power of positive affirmations in your life. Never let distracting, intrusive, or unexpected events dominate your thoughts or behavior. Rise above it to achieve your goals and dreams in life.

It's amazing how powerful and distracting intrusions and interruptions can be. Rarely are they crucial or vital, yet they can easily take over, derailing our focus and causing us to take our eyes off our goals. However, they will happen, and when they do, you need to have the strength to say "NO." If it can be dealt with later, then deal with it later and stay focused on what is more important *NOW*.

Some distractions can be proactively prevented. For example, your phone can serve as a major disruption if you are trying to get something important done. But contrary to popular belief, your phone doesn't own you; you own your phone! This means you have the power to silence it—or turn it off completely—whenever you choose. One of the biggest blessings of modern inventions like voice mail and text messaging is you don't have to feel like you must always answer every call or respond immediately to every message the moment you receive it. You can turn your phone off when necessary and then turn it back on to check your messages later on after you have finished more important work.

There are times, of course, that require our immediate attention, such as if your child falls and injures him/herself. But there is much we can do to

---

[14] Woolbert, C.H. & Smith, J.F. (Reviser). *Fundamentals of Speech: A Textbook of Delivery*, Third Edition. New York, NY: Harper & Brothers Publishers. Page 40.
[15] Ibid. Page 26.

limit distractions and prevent emergencies. If we will take these preventative measures, we will have more time to focus on tasks that are *important* rather than *urgent*.

When you make a commitment and then fail to follow through, you need to take personal responsibility and own up to the fact that it wasn't the distraction or interruption that kept you from your desired success, it was the choices you made when the interruptions invaded your space. Personal responsibility demands that we be brutally honest with ourselves, which can be a hard pill to swallow. But if we want to achieve our goals, me must be willing to take our medicine in this regard!

While many variables contribute to the results we get in our lives, the single biggest factor is *YOUR CHOICES*. Life is about making Choices. From the moment we open our eyes in the morning until the moment we drift off to sleep at night, we are making decisions that will affect our behavior, mood, feelings, experiences, and results. Developing the maturity to admit to yourself when you made a bad decision and then taking the responsibility to rectify it is not easy. But it can be done. Indeed, it *must* be done if we seek to achieve our important goals in life. You can avoid the "Blame Game" by practicing taking full responsibility for the results you get in your life, regardless of the variables at play over which you cannot fully control.

To illustrate a "curveball" that came to me outside of my control, I recently came down with walking pneumonia in the middle of writing this book. My symptoms included a fever and what seemed to be an endless and exhausting cough. It was physically debilitating! During times when I was feverish, I didn't have the desire or strength to do any writing. Fortunately, I had been writing for as many as six (6) hours a day (instead of my goal of only 2) before I got sick. This helped make up for my inability to write for two hours during the days I was sick. When things like sickness invade your well laid-out plans, the worst thing you can do is beat yourself up. Sometimes there will be circumstances beyond your control that can disrupt your schedule and/or energy to the point that you are unable to move forward for a time. Recognize these legitimate exceptions and affirm to yourself that everything is going to be okay and that you will get back on track as soon as the crisis has passed.

Now, let's get back to puzzles...

One evening, totally unexpectedly, my grandson, Andrew (in his early 20s) knocked on my door. I'm always touched when a busy young adult takes time to come and visit me. He has come unannounced before and together we assembled a 300-piece puzzle. After a lovely visit for about 20-minutes, he asked if I had another puzzle we could tackle. I did. It was a 300-piece Thomas Kincade painting called *Mountain Chapel* and we got right to work. I silently wondered what this particular puzzle would teach me.

We agreed that I would sort and assemble the edges while he put like-colored pieces in groups on the table and started working on the sky. I thought it was particularly thoughtful of him to face the puzzle so it was right-side-up for me, something I thanked him for. I was impressed at how well he was getting the sky together despite having to do it upside down and let him know I thought he was brilliant and doing amazingly well with it upside down. He looked at me with a big grin and said, "Grandma, the box-picture of the puzzle is facing me upside down, so it's not at all difficult to figure out." I smiled back, and with an equally large grin, replied, "Duh!" If you want to get something done right and it is upside down, then you are likely to see things better if your guide, map, or, in this case, the picture showing what the puzzle is supposed to look like is *also* upside down.

Have you ever been upset with, confused by, or at your wits end trying to figure out why a two- or four-year old child is behaving a certain way? In our older, adult brain, we know and understand a lot more than toddlers and small children. Such tots haven't lived long enough to see things the way we do, so if we really want to understand their behavior, we must look at the situation upside down, or in other words think back to when we were young and how we were likely to behave under related conditions at a similar age.

If you find you are having an unusually difficult time doing something, ask yourself: is this a situation where I need to look at it *upside down*? If so, then take the opportunity to consider things from a different, more accurate, perspective. It might just make all the difference in how you see and respond to the situation.

When you think about it, *turning it upside down* is sort of what you do when you write and repeat a positive affirmation. Instead of perceiving and affirming a negative result in your puzzle or life—which, as human beings, we tend to naturally fall prey to—positive affirmations allow us to "Turn it Upside Down" whereby we consciously *change* our focus by intentionally perceiving and affirming a different, more positive result instead. The results of this simple, yet powerful practice can be truly MAGICAL! So, what do you have to lose to try it? The answer is: you have *nothing* to lose. So, why not give it a shot… right now!

My Positive Affirmation

_____

_____

_____

_____

_____

I will place this affirmation: _____.

I will repeat this affirmation _____ times per day until I have realized it in my life.

_____
Signed

_____
Date

Chapter 10

NOW WHAT?

You have just completed a beautiful puzzle.

So…what happens next?

I've heard more than one old sage testify that what really counts and matters in life is not so much the destination, but the process or journey. I may not be a "sage," but my age (77) certainly qualifies me as "old" and I do have a lot of experience with both puzzling and life, so I can bear testimony this is true. This realization should not diminish nor negate the satisfaction and joy of ends results, but rather enhance and magnify the value of the experience and adventure experienced along the way.

After completing a puzzle, it is nice to sit at your table for a minute and joyfully survey the finished product. You know—just sit there and soak it all in for a little while. It is, after all, akin to a work of art, assembled by your own hand by virtue of sweat equity invested over time. Chances are you faced difficult and frustrating moments along the way, but you persevered through all of them to realize your objective.

CONGRATULATIONS!

You have finally reached the summit of puzzle assembly. The question now becomes: so now what? You have accomplished your mission, but sooner or later you have to free up your kitchen table for eating, working, etc. If you don't disassemble the puzzle, you can't do another puzzle, or anything else for that matter, unless you have an extra table lying around.

In this interim period of consideration, I invite you to consider what you learned from the experience, and how those lessons relate to *real* life—and more specifically to your life. To amplify this process, you may even want to jot down some thoughts that come to your mind on this important subject. A great place to record such thoughts is in a personal diary or journal. When you have finished that, here are a few suggestions of what to do next.

1. **Let it just be there for a few days.**
   It's taken a lot of time to complete your puzzle and you've earned the right to bask in the glory and satisfaction of just looking at and enjoying the fruits of your labors for a little while. You may also want to show your work to someone else before you disassemble it and return the pieces to the box.

2. **Undo the puzzle and put it back in the box.**
   You could wrap it up as a white elephant gift at a Christmas party, or gift it to a friend you know would enjoy assembling it as you did.

3. **Store it to be reassembled another time by kids, grandchildren, friends, or neighbors who come to visit.**
   You'll actually enjoy doing it again, especially if you have someone else to share it with.

4. **If it was an ok experience, but you have no desire to ever reassemble it, give the puzzle away to a friend or a second-hand store.**
   This will provide someone else, perhaps someone with limited funds for purchasing puzzles, the chance to share in the same joy you experienced.

5. **If you really love it, consider framing it.**
First, Mod Podge it with a paint brush. Mod Podge can be purchased online or at a craft store such as *Michaels* or *Hobby Lobby*. It dries quickly, allowing you to pick up the puzzle as if it were a piece of card board. Now you can take it with you to the store and match it to the perfect frame. Mod Podge comes in either matte or shiny finish. If you are going to put glass over the puzzle, I highly recommend using the matte finish, as the glass will create enough shine of its own. Without glass, the shiny finish provides a beautiful glossy appearance.

One day, I had another grandson come to visit. He chose a 300-piece puzzle from my collection in the closet. It was a mountain scene with a creek and a couple of deer in it. Knowing how much he liked this picture, I Mod Podged and framed it and then gave it to him for Christmas. He was in college and had just moved into a new apartment. Trust me when I say his walls needed help! Plus, we did it together so when I'm dead and gone perhaps he will remember the fun time we had assembling it together.

6. **Choose an appropriate frame**
More than 20 years ago I was visiting my son Paul in Spokane, Washington. He had meetings in Coeur d'Alene, Idaho, and I accompanied him. Before heading to his meetings, Paul dropped me off at a beautiful place near a large, multistory hotel. Inside were several shops for me to investigate. I went first into one called the *Hidden Cottage*. It wasn't a very large store but I spent about three hours checking out every nook and cranny. After an hour of wandering through this mini-wonderland, I noted one Thomas Kincade painting called "Christmas Memories." It was in an old European style frame and it really spoke to me. It wasn't cheap, but I was so moved by it that I decided to purchase it.

After about my fourth lap around the entire store, I noted two other paintings just like it, but they were in different frames. One was in a sort of "Western" style frame and the other rested in a simple dark mahogany.

I was stunned. After four trips around the shop, I had failed to notice the other two paintings, which were exactly the same, except for their frames. Only one of these spoke to me. I learned a great lesson that day: *How you frame something makes all the difference.*

> **How you frame something makes all the difference.**

There was no question I loved the painting, yet I only noticed one out of the three paintings and it was all because of how it was framed. When I got the painting home, I discovered I had two other pictures in the same frame. Here is the grouping I made. As you can probably guess, it's the era of frame that won me over.

So, how does framing something relate to real life?

I remember when I was a manager at a women's clothing store called *Talbots*. When a customer would ask me my opinion about an article of clothing or outfit she was trying on, I would always be honest while striving to frame my comments in a positive light. For example, I might say something like: "the style is fabulous and complements your build, but I don't think it's your best color." Or, "The color is terrific on you, but I don't think the style compliments your body type and build." The point is: in order for something to be right for you, it needs to possess *feng shui* (remember that term?) But it also needs to feel right, or in other words, make you feel comfortable and confident.

I once had the opportunity to visit the home of Dennis Weaver, a 20th century Hollywood actor who famously played "Chester" on *Gunsmoke* in the 1950s-1970s. In the later 1990s, he gave my husband and our two youngest kids a tour of his unique, southwestern style home in Colorado. It was a remarkable structure (mansion) and ideally suited to his personal preferences and style. Yet I remember thinking how much it clashed with my style and how I would never feel comfortable or at peace in that style of home. While I greatly appreciate what he had created for himself, it just didn't jive with my own styles and preferences.

Remember, we were created so that we might have joy, so don't fall into the latest fads, trends or ideas simply because they are "new" or considered "trendy," "cool," or "popular." What matters to you is what is most important. If you end up choosing a mat (not to be confused with matte) to surround your puzzle in the frame, you will discover there are multiple options that work and can beautifully enhance the puzzle and the room in which you choose to display the puzzle.

Speaking of displays, there is never just one way to present something. You will discover that different colors (or frames) can work, but depending on what you choose, the picture itself will take on a different look. So, evaluate which look you prefer and why you like it best. Then, before deciding, look at all the options because there will always be one that speaks to you more than the others. If it doesn't speak to you, you probably need to keep looking for just the right mat and frame.

7. **Hang it in your home.**
   I did a puzzle of Jesus with four little children. The picture really spoke to me. If I bought an oil reprint of this painting it would have cost me hundreds of dollars. The puzzle itself was just under $20, so when I completed it, the expense involved was my time and the frame, which of course would vary depending on the frame I chose. People couldn't even tell it was a puzzle until they got really close. It was beautiful and provided me with a lovely wall painting that really spoke to me without having to spend a small fortune to obtain the same image.

8. **Give a framed puzzle to someone you know will love and appreciate the picture.**
   They will likely treasure it more than a regular picture because of their knowledge that you played a significant role in its creation.

9. **Use your imagination.**
   There are more places to put finished puzzles than on the wall. Suppose you are big on ocean scenes or old-fashioned ships. Perhaps your entire bedroom or office reflects this theme. Take an appropriate table, put the Mod Podged work of art on this table and buy some glass to cover the table. The picture you love is always there looking up at you while being protected from wear and tear. You can actually buy puzzles as small as 4 x 6 inches or smaller, allowing you to make coasters or hot plates; you can then buy plastic that can handle heat. Suffice it to say, there are endless possibilities; just put your thinking cap on and get creative. They even make circular and oval-shaped puzzles, which provide a unique variation on the traditional rectangular-shaped ones.

10. **Sell your framed work.**
    Look for puzzles of famous pictures from the old masters like Rembrandt or Constable, or perhaps more recently renowned artists like Thomas Kincade. Assemble them, frame them, and then sell them. Most folks

can't afford originals, or even prints for that matter. A framed puzzle of these works looks fabulous and is much more affordable. You can savor the satisfaction of enjoying the puzzling process and then of knowing someone else will be blessed to display the finished product in their home.

You have probably lived long enough to know and understand when something "speaks" to you. When I finally got back to Utah to hang my Thomas Kincade puzzle with two other framed items I really liked, I was stunned—flabbergasted actually—to discover that the frames surrounding the other two pictures were exactly the same as the one I just fell in love with at the Hidden Cottage. I had no idea! This illustrated to me how innate our personal preferences are. It also taught me that there is wisdom in our instincts.

Chapter II
FROM FEAR TO FAITH

From Fear to Faith

A dear friend gave me a 500-piece puzzle for Christmas called *From Fear to Faith*. The title couldn't be more perfect or pertinent as it reminded me that faith moves you forward while fear holds you back. I felt confident I could do it and wasn't afraid to try, but I also knew it wouldn't be fast or easy because there were so many black, reds, browns and greens. When the individual pieces were spread out on my table it was extremely difficult to determine exactly what color each piece really was.

From Fear to Faith in process

I loved the picture, and as you can see by the photograph, when the puzzle was still in progress, I got the lighter and more varied colors put together first. Once this part of the puzzle was done, I found myself once again employing the "Hit and Miss" strategy, which can be frustrating. But such frustration also makes it even more satisfying when you finally find a piece's rightful place.

Oh, the joy of that!

As you can see from the picture, I put white paper underneath parts of the puzzle that still needed to be completed. I did this because the table I was doing the puzzle on was dark and made it challenging to see the other dark pieces.

We live in a fast-paced society and era. You can drive up to so many places of business today and get what you want without having to even go inside. We have drive-up windows for fast food, banking, medical prescriptions, and the list goes on. And if you don't want to get in your car at all, you can order what you want online and like magic it will appear right on your doorstep! We have become a society of "fast" everything and I think our collective patience has waned as a result.

Modern marvels of efficiency and speed, amazing and convenient though they may be, do not negate our need for patience. Patience comes in handy in all sorts of different life scenarios, and puzzling is certainly one of them. For example, there were days when I only managed to assemble three or four pieces in a particularly challenging puzzle. Those days were always discouraging. But I learned several life lessons in the process.

First, I know if I stick to it, I will eventually have a breakthrough because I've done equally difficult puzzles before. On the other hand, I also understand that if I set my expectations at an unreasonable timetable for completion, I'm only setting myself up for a frustrating, laborious and discouraging experience. As such, it's usually best to not limit yourself to a specific timeframe to complete a puzzle. It's often counterproductive to try and force time when puzzling because unless you have the time to work on it all day, *Life Happens*!

Remember your need for Variety? Well, amidst your life and all of its responsibilities, you might say that puzzling is one of those interesting and fun diversions that provides you with *variety*, which is truly the "Spice of Life."

Part of living a balanced life is scheduling some "Fun Time" and "Down Time" in addition to the many things you *have to do*. Doing so gives you a break, affording you the opportunity to rest, regroup, listen to your favorite music, contemplate/ponder/reflect, etc. Healthy breaks allow you to return to your daily life renewed and refreshed. This strategy of balance not only works in assembling a puzzle, but in living your life as well.

After taking a break for the evening, I returned to my *From Fear to Faith* puzzle the next morning. And guess what? Viewing it from a standing position I immediately placed four pieces where they were meant to be. Go figure! Why couldn't I see things this clearly the night before? The answer is: because whether you are puzzling or doing something else that takes a lot of focus, after a while you reach a point where your productivity plummets. Hunger, fatigue, anxiety, boredom—there are various contributing factors that lead to this feeling I refer to as being "Brain Dead." As human beings, we do have our limits. When we cease to be productive, it usually means we need to take a break and do something different for a while. It might just be time to retire to bed for the night. Or perhaps you could go on a walk, take a nap, play an instrument, do some cleaning or cooking, or watch a video or television program you enjoy. Taking this break renews and revitalizes your energy and perspective and helps to invite the success you are seeking.

There are always signs or signals that tell you *when* you need to take a break or change course. For example, last night I worked on my puzzle for an entire hour yet only found two pieces that fit. This extended period of unproductivity signaled to me it was time to take a break and do something different. Before doing so, however, I stood up and carefully looked at the puzzle from a different angle and perspective because this sometimes helps me reach a breakthrough. When that didn't help, I knew for sure it was time for me to take a break.

Call it "Puzzle Block," if you will, and it's a real phenomenon—just like "Writer's Block." Your inability to make progress is often your body and mind's way of letting you know it is time to stop. The specific signs may be different for you than they are for me. Just be aware of your progress; then, when you stop progressing, listen to your gut, take charge, and take that needed break with the knowledge and confidence that when you return with a fresh body, mind, and outlook, you will eventually make the desired breakthrough.

Think about the last time you had to choose a product from among 10 or more options. For example, you are buying a car and there are a dozen different colors to choose from. Now think about the last time you had to choose a product from among five or fewer options.

Which choice is easier?

The answer, of course, is an option among *fewer* choices. Simply stated, fewer options simplifies decision-making processes.

> **The more options you have, the more difficult your choice becomes.**

If you don't believe this, try holding five different colors of lollipops in front of a child with instructions to choose only one. Then offer the child only two options and see which choice is made more quickly. Rarely will the kid choose faster when confronted with *more* options.

Another example of this involved a gentleman I know who is past fifty years old. When asked why he wasn't married, his answer was: "I think if I lived in the country, where there were fewer women available, I'd probably already be married. But there are so many choices here in the city that I keep thinking there might be another one out there that is better."

He might be right!

This may be a little off-topic, but I sometimes hear those who are looking for a long-term marriage partner asking the question: "Can I live with this person?" Maybe it is just the romantic in me, but I think a better question is: "Can I live without this person?"

When we are making decisions about which puzzle to do, questions you might ask yourself include: "Am I drawn to it?" or "Does it speak to me?" When you've decided you want to get a puzzle and give it a shot, I highly recommend you make certain decisions before you even go to the store, or look online, where there will be dozens, scores, or perhaps even hundreds or thousands of different options. These early decisions can involve how many pieces you want in your puzzle, whether you want animated or natural scenes, and whether you want a puzzle by a famous artist or someone less well known. This will help you narrow your choices and make your final decision easier when shopping.

Another variable to consider is how much money you are able and/or willing to pay for a puzzle. Like any product, puzzles come in a range of different prices. If you have a list and a plan of what you are looking for, you will save time and money, which always feels good.

Take for example this painting of Thomas Kincaid's "Mountain Chapel" (see next page). I actually have the real McCoy (a print) of this painting hanging in my bedroom, but at a thousand times the cost of the puzzle. So, I decided to Mod Podge and frame it; perhaps just a cheap knock off of the real thing, but it is much more affordable and looks almost as good!

I first chose a style of frame that "spoke" to me, and of course adds to and compliments this puzzle. Then I chose the perfect mat to surround it as a frame within the frame. Anything worth framing deserves a mat; it's classier and delivers a better overall result. The mat is the hardest part of getting it right because multiple options may work. The question for you is, of all the available options, which one makes the picture say "Voile" or "Shazam!" To me, *voile* or *shazam* are two ways of saying "magical" in an even spicier way. And for me, SHAZAM is always the goal!

There will always be more than just one right shade or hue. With the variety of colors in this painting (puzzle) as a guide, check out multiple options

PUZZLED

Mountain Chapel *by* Thomas Kincaid

and then select the one that best enhances the picture. If it's a different frame, then the mat will likely also be different. The color of a mat dictates what you want to highlight. Is it the sky, the chapel, the river, the flowers etc.? When your effort delivers "Shazam" you can almost hear the puzzle saying: "Ah yes, that's the one, thank you for helping me look my BEST!"

Over time, you'll discover that certain colors look better with the frame than others. The important thing is to choose what rings your chimes without taking anything away from the main event, which is the puzzle (or any picture needing a frame for that matter).

Chapter 12

FINAL THOUGHTS

Earlier, I discussed the difference between the left and right sides of our brains. The best human creations are often those that use both sides of our brains—the analytic and creative sides working harmoniously and synergistically together. When this balance occurs, *feng shui* is achieved and magic can occur. If we only use one side of our brain to figure things out or make a decision, the results are likely to be inferior to those decisions made utilizing both sides.

I've come to the conclusion that this phenomenon is one of the reasons why some relationships and marriages are more successful than others. If a right-brained woman and a left-brained man (or vice versa) truly listen to one another's thoughts, ideas, feelings, and perspectives, the synergy created between them can be immensely satisfying and massively productive. I believe the same principle holds true for friendships and work relationships. Differing perspectives working together in harmony create a broader and more holistic understanding of a situation and can lead to better decision-making.

Figuring out a puzzle or figuring out your life really boils down to the choices you make. Life is about making *CHOICES*. From the moment we open our eyes in the morning until the moment we drift off to sleep at night, we are making decisions that will affect our behavior, mood, feelings, experiences, and results. As a Certified Household Manager and accredited Interior Decorator, I can testify that how you arrange furniture, colors, and other ornamentation in your home or workplace has a powerful effect on how you feel, function, and operate. To aid in this edification and enjoyment, I encourage you to arrange your surroundings in a way that enhances both your puzzling and life experiences. In my experience, the greatest happiness is not found in the results you get from an undertaking, but from the journey that got you there. The journey is where the real joy occurs.

So… enjoy the *JOURNEY!*

While there are many *external* variables that influence how we react in our lives, always remember that your own *internal* strength and freedom to choose your *responses* ultimately trumps all. With this in mind, I hope you can get excited about your future and the personal power you have to control your thoughts, speech, actions, and ultimately the long-term direction of your life.

In a sense, the steps to successfully completing a puzzle and successfully living your life are similar. Now that you know this, I encourage you to continue to allow your experiences assembling puzzles to inform your life experiences and decisions.

We all make decisions and choices that determine the path we follow. How you approach a puzzle and how you approach life is really no different. Are you discouraged? Frustrated? Invigorated? Miserable? Happy? Overwhelmed? Satisfied? Angry? Feel like giving up?

These are all emotions you are likely to feel as you tackle a puzzle. They are also the same feelings you will encounter in life—many times over. As puzzles teach you what you like, don't like, enjoy, thrive on, etc., you can easily transfer your newfound understandings to real life and its endless obstacles and opportunities.

Most importantly, recognize that if you are not happy with where you are or what you are doing, YOU have the *power to change* by altering your attitude, your environment, your perceptions, and your approach to a situation. When all is said and done, your choices determine your outcomes and results.

Have the courage to change and eliminate what you don't like, grasp and pursue the things you want and do like, and accept it when you make mistakes, while exercising determination to gradually improve throughout your life.

Work hard… yes! But also remember to take needed and meaningful breaks as required. And don't forget to consciously look at things from a different perspective when you are stuck. I am always amazed how one day I can't seem to find any pieces that fit properly together and then the next day I can put ten pieces together in a matter of minutes. So, if you give up on that dark and gloomy day when you are struggling, you will never get to that bright and cheerful day where everything is sailing smoothly; and believe me when I say: it's worth the wait!

As I've mentioned before, "Puzzle Block" is a real phenomenon. So are "Life Blocks." But just as you can take steps to break through "Puzzle Blocks" you can find solutions to navigating over, under, around, or through "Life Blocks" as well. Consider the following list of possible "Life Blocks" you may be facing…

- **Fatigue**
- **Feelings of inadequacy**
- **Biting off more than you can chew**
- **Distractions & interruptions**
- **Self-imposed pressures**
- **Hate your job**
- **Poor self-image / low self-esteem**
- **Comparing yourself to others**
- **Unexpected health challenges**
- **Financial difficulties**
- **Lack of faith in yourself**
- **Fear of failure**

With these items in mind, write down all the things currently holding you back.

1. _____
2. _____
3. _____
4. _____
5. _____
6. _____
7. _____

FEAR is often what holds many of us back. If FEAR is holding you back, consider the following gems of wisdom…

> "The cave you fear to enter often holds the treasure that you seek."
>
> Joseph Campbell

> You meet Grace when you face your *fears*.

> "You never know how strong you are until strong is your only choice."
>
> Bob Marley

With these maxims in mind, what are some ACTIONS you could take beginning *today* to help you become unpuzzled in your life and get back on a trajectory towards living your dreams?

Action 1: _____

Action 2: _____

Action 3: _____

The Parable of the Fly

One night around 11:00 p.m., I made some of my famous fudge. This homemade baked good was a bestselling item at my little gift shop, *Polly's Parlor*, in Monticello, Utah, that I owned and operated in the early 2000s.

Accompanying me that evening was a friendly (annoying) house fly. He seemed to enjoy being right there beside me as I made my fudge—despite numerous efforts to shoo him away (approach #1). When my shooing efforts failed, I started running out of hair spray trying to asphyxiate the little stinker (approach #2). When this second approach failed, I realized I might have to break down and buy a fly swatter because past experience has taught me that they are very effective.

The minute I got out of bed the next morning, my annoying little pest made his presence known again with the sound of that irritating bzzzzzzzzzz. At this point, I could hear in my mind the words of my older brother Denis saying: "Just remember, you are smarter than the fly." Pausing to ponder the subject of flies, I decided to ask Siri about the life span of a fly. Siri replied back that a fly has a lifespan of 30-40 days. She then proceeded to explain how a fly can lay multiple eggs in that period of time. If it were only a few days, I figured I could accept his company and just let him die a natural death, but thoughts of an entire fly family taking up residence in my home for weeks-on-end was simply not acceptable. One way or another, it was time to terminate the fly!

Rummaging through my "Everything Drawer," I found some sticky mouse paper on which I put a wee bit of peanut butter, thinly spread across the paper, in hopes the fly would get caught on the sticky mouse paper in an attempt to sample the peanut butter (approach #3). Knowing I really am smarter than the fly, I was determined to win this battle without having to get in my car, drive to the store, and purchase a fly swatter. Nevertheless, it started to dawn on me how ridiculous it was that this little creature was taking up so much of my time, energy, and thought processes. Why was I letting something so small exercise so much power over me?

At this point, I began to laugh! I figured I'm either losing it or I have a healthy ability to see the humor in my fly drama. Life experience has taught me that laughter is always a good way to handle these sorts of situations. After all, laughter really is like medicine for both the body, mind, and spirit.

Resuming my determination to win this battle of wits with my fly friend, an actual friend suggested I put a dish of sugar and water on the counter in hopes that the fly would be drawn to the dish and then drown in the water. I thought it was a great idea so I prepared the aforementioned concoction (approach #4) and placed it in the kitchen next to my sticky mouse paper covered in peanut butter. At this point, I was feeling extra confident and sassy; I was going to win this battle!

Later in the day, however, I saw no results from either remedy. On top of that, I touched the mouse paper, which also managed to attach itself to both a paper catalog *and* my fingers. I'll tell you what, that mouse paper is brutally sticky and wouldn't let go of either, which further infuriated me. At this point, the thought crossed my mind that maybe I *was* going to *lose* this battle—definitely not a thought to give in to. Getting the mouse paper off of my beautiful Christmas catalog was an adventure, and removing it from my fingers was tricky as well.

Maybe if I just left the front door open for a while, the fly would realize he was safer outside and choose to leave (approach #5), but then there is an added risk that other members of the fly's extended family may choose to come in out of the heat, and *that* was definitely not an acceptable option!

Despite my growing frustration and irritation with this wee little winged devil, I had to remind myself that I am 77 years old; *this* was not my first fly-rodeo! I had learned from past fly encounters that I'm pretty deadly with a "swatter." I know they work, so after several days of zero success in curbing my intruder's shenanigans, I finally broke down, drove to the store, and returned home armed with my new fly swatter (approach #6). I confess I walked through my front door a bit self-satisfied and smug, knowing I was destined to finally find success and claim victory in this battle of attrition. My success and victory in battle was only a matter of time now.

With fly swatter-in-hand, I finally triumphed! The question remained, however: why would I spend so much time and frustration on so many methods—five (5) to be exact—when I knew all along that a swatter would do the job? And even more so than this, why would I allow a pesky fly to dominate my living space, sap my energy, and leave me feeling so powerless for days on end when I already knew *exactly* what would work all along?

At moments like this in life, I am reminded of a pithy and humorous three-word quote from the famous comedian, Brian Regan, who once quipped: "Human beings man!" Indeed… to err is human; but sometimes, we can sure make ridiculous decisions and cause ourselves a lot of unnecessary grief even though we know better!

Age and experience teach and mentor us. If asked the question, "would you go back to your youth?" Or, "If given the chance, would you return to your twenties or thirties?"

To this question I can answer honestly and unequivocally "No." Why? Because if I returned to my youth, I would lose all the life lessons I painstakingly earned throughout my 40s, 50s, 60s, and 70s. Those decades provided me with blessings, experiences, lessons learned, and acquired wisdom that cannot be bought—no matter how much money you have to spend.

The point of the story is this: Always be willing to learn the lessons that a puzzle (or life opportunity) offers to you. Then, if the experience proves unsuccessful, isn't worthwhile, or doesn't give you joy, be willing to let your *old* plan go and embrace a new approach. It's okay to ponder, evaluate, and recognize when it's time to let go of something or someone and not spend any more time or energy with a particular puzzle, project, or person. Such a move does not make you a quitter; it merely means you have made an informed decision in the best interest of your long-term health, joy, and peace.

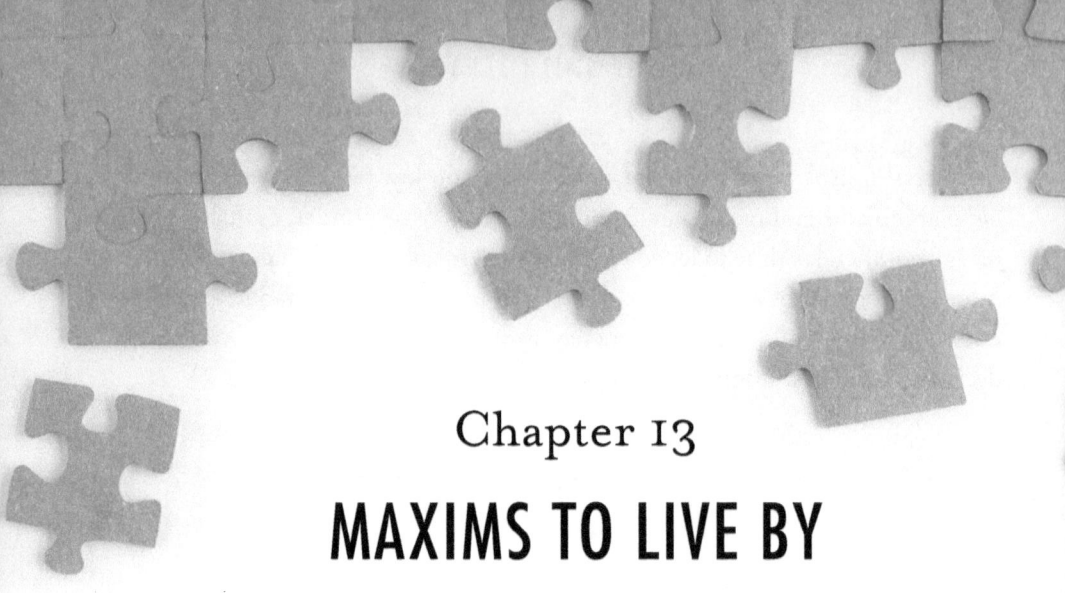

Chapter 13

MAXIMS TO LIVE BY

If you take nothing else away from this book, I hope you will remember that your life is the result of the CHOICES you make every single day. So, learn all you can about how to make wise choices. Doing so will help you to live without those pesky regrets that tend to cling onto us like honey on a pancake. Strive with all your heart to make choices that positively affect you and deliver wonder, bliss, delight, peace, and joy.

Throughout this book I have included a variety of different maxims—or gems of thought. Some of them come in the form of questions; these provide you with points to ponder. Others are statements of counsel and advice which, if heeded, will bless your life and relationships immensely. I would like to end this book with a concluding list of these gems of thought for your consideration and reflection. Some of them are of my own concoction. Others I gleaned from my parents or others. I hope they help you in your life as much as they have helped me in mine. You will recognize many of these because a lot of them were included as boxed quotes throughout this book.

Maxims to Live By

1. Know why you are doing what you are doing. What purpose does it serve?
2. Don't always believe everything you see in print or on the news. "Trust, but verify!"[16]
3. Faith is action based on true principles.
4. Life happens and we must deal with it, but it sure helps to have accurate information!
5. Even if a piece fits, it may be in the wrong place.
6. A second pair of eyes often sees what we don't.
7. "Insanity is doing the same things over and over again and expecting different results." *~ Albert Einstein*
8. "Adversity is the diamond dust that heaven polishes her jewels with." *~ Thomas Carlyle*
9. The first time it's the dog's fault; the second time it's yours.
10. How you frame something makes all the difference.
11. The more options you have, the more difficult your choice becomes.
12. "He who conquers himself is the mightiest warrior." *~ Confucius*
13. "Next to the bestowal of life itself, the right to direct that life is God's greatest gift to mankind." *~ David O. McKay*
14. Learn from past experiences. Don't make the same mistakes over and over again.
15. Own up to the choices you make. Never play the blame game.
16. Listen to your body, sometimes it knows more than you give it credit for.
17. Results come from choices YOU make. So, choose carefully!
18. Ends can be terrific moments, but *real joy* comes during the *JOURNEY*.
19. You have the power to change course, but only when you recognize and acknowledge your need to change.
20. Know when to stop and do something else.

---

[16] Often attributed to Ronald Reagan

21. "A change is as good as a rest." ~ *Winston Churchill*
22. JOY is greatest when we can, through our knowledge, benefit someone else with that knowledge.
23. Knowing who you are and what your talents and gifts are increases your ability to make good choices.
24. Sharing your experience and knowledge can make a worthwhile difference to others.
25. "You never know how strong you are until strong is your only choice." ~ *Bob Marley*
26. Doing difficult things makes you stronger and reveals what you are capable of.
27. "Knowing others is Intelligence but knowing yourself is true Wisdom." ~ *Lao Tsu*
28. "Mastering others is Strength, but mastering yourself is true Power." ~ *Lao Tsu*
29. "Knowing yourself is the beginning of all Wisdom." ~ *Aristotle*
30. "Things will work out in the end. If they haven't worked out yet, it isn't the end." [17]
31. Look in the mirror and choose to be the architect of your own life.
32. Your life is a reflection of your views, habits, attitudes, beliefs, thoughts, fears, worries, and perceptions. All these things come together to build and shape who you *are* and what you *become*.
33. No one can teach you anything unless you choose to learn. It is a choice.
34. Pay attention to all you learn and be careful with what you do with that knowledge.
35. Enjoy the Journey.
36. When progress is stifled and you cease to move forward, do something different until you are restored.

---

[17] Attributed to Tracy McMillan

37. Self-awareness is required in leading yourself to the life you envision for yourself.
38. Positive behavior and actions elevate both you and those around you.
39. "Self-awareness is crucial for all levels of success." ~ *Daniel Goleman*
40. You must first lead yourself before you can lead others.
41. "It is not enough just to be good. You must be good for something. You must contribute good to the world. The world must be a better place for your presence." ~ *Gordon Hinckley*
42. Your inability to make progress is your body's way of letting you know it's time to stop and take a break.
43. "That which does not kill you makes you stronger."
44. "Dost thou love life? Then do not squander time. For that's the stuff life is made of" ~ *Benjamin Franklin*
45. All work and no play makes Jack a dull boy.
46. All play and no work makes Jack a sad, unproductive, and unhappy boy.
47. Grab the bull by the horns. Be serious and intentional with your choices.
48. "If we don't try, we don't do, and if we don't do, then what's life all about?" ~ From the movie, *Shenandoah*.
49. Never underestimate the power of example.
50. "The jump is so frightening between where I am and where I want to be, because of all I may become, I will close my eyes and leap." ~ *Mary Anne Radmacher*
51. Remember, God doesn't give you anything you can't handle.
52. "God always answers prayers. Sometimes He says 'Yes' sometimes He says 'No' and sometimes He says 'Wait a while.'" ~ *Darlene Andrus*
53. Hasty resolutions rarely deliver the best outcomes.
54. It's easier to make good choices than to suffer the consequences of poor choices.
55. Sometimes you must rise up and take a stand; other times it's best to go with the flow.

56. Goals are good, but it's not always wise to limit your time in reaching them.
57. Variety is the spice of life.
58. "For God hath not given us the spirit of fear, but of power, and of love, and of a sound mind." ~ *2 Timothy 1:7*
59. He who asks the questions controls the conversation.
60. Man is that he might have JOY. ~ 2 Nephi 2:25 (*The Book of Mormon*)
61. "You can do the impossible, because you have been through the unimaginable." ~ *Christina Rasmussen*
62. Let your faith be bigger than your fears.
63. If something is too difficult, we become afraid and discouraged.
64. Different does not mean defective.
65. "When life gives you lemons, make lemonade."
66. Two wrongs never make a right.
67. Write and repeat manageable Positive Affirmations to help you reach your goals.
68. You meet Grace when you face your fears.
69. "Life is the art of drawing with an eraser." ~ *John Gardner*
70. "Art is not what you see, but what you make others see." ~ *Edgar Degas*
71. Fear is the habit of anticipating the worst.
72. "Duty makes us do things well, but love makes us do them beautifully." ~ *Zig Ziglar*
73. "If you can't say something nice, don't say anything at all" ~ *My Mother*
74. "Pretty is as pretty does." ~ *My Mother*
75. I can do anything with God on my side.
76. The greatest joy comes from sharing what you know to help others on their way. So, don't keep things to yourself that can and will bless and edify them.
77. "A leader is often his [or her] own best teacher." ~ *Winston Churchill*

Well, I determined to not have any more of these gems than my present age, so it's time to stop at 77! Once again, I hope you find as much wisdom and inspiration in these maxims as I have. Moving forward, I encourage you to avoid looking backwards and stewing over your past life. Instead, learn from your experiences and forge ahead into an ever-brighter future. Claim your own voice, build on all you've gained in your travels, and be willing to share your wisdom so others might also thrive. And when you become *puzzled*, which you surely will from time-to-time, I invite you to return to this book. Perhaps you will find just the nugget you need to get you back on track, whether in the midst of *puzzling*, or in the midst of life.

May you enjoy your journey!

Appendix

PUZZLE PICTURE GALLERY

Since the beginning of the pandemic, I have assembled more than 30 puzzles. And Heaven only knows how many puzzles I've completed in my lifetime. In this appendix, I would like to share a sampling of my favorites finished over the past three years.

The Bicycle

Chinese House in process

Chinese House Complete

PUZZLED

Colonial Williamsburg with Missing Piece

Cottage with Missing Piece

Country Store in process

Country Store complete

Eagle in process

Eagle in process

Eagle Mountain box and pieces

Eagle Mountain in process

Gingerbread House in process

Gingerbread House complete

Horse & Carriage in process

Horse and Carriage

Jesus and the Children

PAULINE SMITH JENSEN

Lake Chalet

PUZZLED

Lake Tahoe

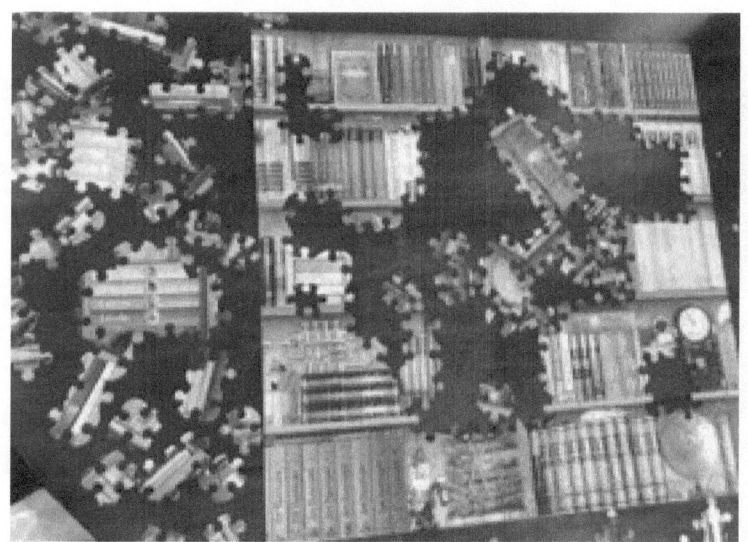
Home Library in process

Home Library complete

PUZZLED

1500-piece Lighthouse Bridge complete with missing piece

PAULINE SMITH JENSEN

Miami Beach in process

Mary & Jesus
Mod Podged & Framed

PUZZLED

Brooklyn Bridge and Manhattan poster and puzzle

Lake Quote in process

Santa Claus

A Parody of Literature in process

A Parody of Literature complete

Cottage Home

Tropical Paradise in process

Tropical Paradise complete

PUZZLED

Tuscan Courtyard in process

Tuscan Courtyard complete

THE END

www.ingramcontent.com/pod-product-compliance
Lightning Source LLC
LaVergne TN
LVHW092049060526
838201LV00047B/1309